uncommon
be extraordinary.

uncommon
games & icebreakers

jim burns
general editor

Published by Gospel Light

Ventura, California, U.S.A.

www.gospellight.com

Printed in the U.S.A.

Library of Congress Cataloging-in-Publication Data

Uncommon games and icebreakers / Jim Burns, general editor ; compiled by Mark Simone and Joel Lusz.

p. cm.

Includes indexes.

ISBN 978-0-8307-4635-4 (trade paper)

1. Church group work with youth. 2. Christian education—Activity programs.

I. Burns, Jim. II. Simone, Mark. III. Lusz, Joel, 1958-

BV4447.U54 2008

268′.433—dc22

2008018809

All definitions are from the *Merriam-Webster* online dictionary.

http://www.merriam-webster.com.

Contributors: Rick Bundschuh, Tom Finley, Matt Harrison, Matt Hoyt, John Moores, Joel Lusz

Tom Patterson, Scott Rubin, Troy Scott, Mark Simone, Kipp Smith, Jonathan Traux

Russ Van Nest, Eric and Starr Wrisley, Diana Weber-Gardner, Daiv Whaley

Caution: Please exercise due caution when using games and icebreakers that are high activity or involve food.

Gospel Light will not be held responsible for any injuries incurred.

1 2 3 4 5 6 7 8 9 10 11 12 13 14 15 / 15 14 13 12 11 10 09 08

Rights for publishing this book outside the U.S.A. or in non-English languages are

administered by Gospel Light Worldwide, an international not-for-profit ministry.

For additional information, please visit www.glww.org, email info@glww.org, or write to Gospel

Light Worldwide, 1957 Eastman Avenue, Ventura, CA 93003, U.S.A.

contents

GAMES

ICEBREAKERS

introduction

Let's face it, most of us are on the lookout for fresh ways to get our youth groups interacting and having fun. This resource not only gives you some of the finest ideas in games and icebreakers known in the youth world, but it is also laid out in the easiest format that I've ever seen!

This resource is divided into easy-to-use categories with icons that tell you instantly how much time you need to prepare, how much cleanup is involved, and even what the gross factor is! We also have an index at the back that gives a brief description of each game so that you don't have to read the whole game to get a quick picture. And to make things easy on you when you're in a hurry, we've devised an index that tells you immediately how much preparation time each activity takes so that when you don't have much time, you know exactly which games or icebreakers to go to and which page they are on.

But this book is not just about fun and games. When a youth group experiences enjoyable times together, the students will be ready to study the Word and participate in the church to a greater extent. So here's to a good time, even at church!

—Jim Burns

a few essential tips

adapt

Read the material, and then ask yourself, *How can I use this with my group?*
What should I add? What should I take away? How can it be adapted for our group?
In other words, change it to fit your students. Change the language. Update
the material. Use the right props and costumes. Adjust. Alter. Tailor-make.
Custom-fit. Modify. Adapt!

use props and costumes

Budget some money for buying costuming paraphernalia—dresses, hats,
boots, jackets, purses, wigs, oversized clothes, telephones, musical instru-
ments, drums, eyeglasses, sports equipment, and so forth. Ask church
members to donate discards or leftovers from garage sales. You'd be amazed
at how many good skit props you can buy at thrift stores, 99¢ stores and
at garage sales with little money. If you're going to do a cowboy skit, get
cowboy hats, boots, holsters, vests and whatever else. Make it more real,
yet outrageous. Something about putting on costumes helps students
loosen up and get into the spirit of the fun.

swallow your pride

If you can't be a fool for Christ, then whose fool are you? Go ahead and
put on the makeup, get hit in the face with a pie, and put mustard under
your arms. Who cares! This is how walls are broken down and relationships are built. Set an example of fun for your students. Go for it!

keep a record

Have you ever wondered if you have already done a skit or played a game
or given a message to the group you're meeting with today? We have tried
to make recordkeeping as simple and convenient as possible. Next to each
activity, message or skit you use, write the date and with which group it
was used. You can also jot down notes for new ideas or suggestions for
adaptations or improvements.

icons used in this book

number

This refers to the number of people who can generally participate in the game or icebreaker. This typically ranges from small groups (less than 10 people) to medium-sized groups (between 10 to 30 people) to any-sized group (more than 30 people).

prep time

This indicates the amount of setup and preparation needed for the game or icebreaker, such as the time needed for measuring, drawing, cooking, and so forth. This does not include the time required for gathering or shopping for the materials needed.

time required

This is the approximate time the activity takes, including the time allotted for giving directions and forming teams, if necessary. (Note: All times are based on semi-cooperative kids.)

playing fields

Some activities work best indoors, some work best outdoors, and some work just as well either way. If there is a special requirement for the game or icebreaker (such as a game that requires snow), it will be listed here as well.

activity levels

This indicates the physical activity level required by the participants. This will typically range from low activity (involves little movement—students generally stay in their seats) to moderate activity (some walking or movement) to high activity (lots of running, movement and noise).

cleanup

Before deciding to do a game or icebreaker, it is always a good idea to know how much cleanup will be involved at the end of the event. Cleanup ranges from none to slight (a little messy—you will need a towel and sponge) to moderate (a multi-toweler with sponges) to heavy (get out the hose and shovels!).

gross factor

This indicates the degree of yuck in the game or icebreaker. Gross factor ranges from none to slight to moderate to disgusting!

GAMES

game \gam\ *n* **1 a** : activity engaged in for diversion or amusement: PLAY. **2 a** : **(1)** A physical or mental competition conducted according to rules with the participants in direct opposition to each other. **(2)** A division of a larger contest. **(3)** Any activity undertaken or regarded as a contest involving rivalry, strategy or struggle.

Games aren't just a fun way to fill time. They have a purpose. Games can build a stronger group and help develop friendships. They put the seriousness of life on hold and give students opportunities to let off steam.

The following games have been divided into two categories. *Group Games* are games in which everyone can participate. *Volunteer Games,* on the other hand, are games in which a few students volunteer to participate while the rest of the group watches. Most of the Volunteer Games have a surprise for at least one of the suckers . . . I mean participants. These may appear to the students to be spontaneous, even though you have taken the time to prepare them. Either way, your students are going to have a great time!

Group Games

group \grüp\ *n* **1** : a number of individuals assembled together or having some unifying relationship.

1

ankle balloon bash

This game works best in a large room or gymnasium.

materials needed

String or narrow gift-wrapping ribbon
Several pairs of scissors
Lots of balloons, at least one for each person

how to play

Provide players with about a three-foot length of string and one balloon. Tell them to blow up their balloons as large as possible (without popping). Then have the players remove their shoes and tie one end of the string to the balloon and the other end to their ankles. The object of the game is to have each student try to pop the other students' balloons without having his or her own balloon popped. When a person's balloon is popped, he or she cannot pop any more balloons and must leave the playing area and sit down. The last person standing with a balloon still around his or her ankle wins.

team variation

Divide students into two teams. Have the two teams line up across from each other on opposite sides of the room. Then, at your signal, have both teams run across the room to the other side. While they are running across the room, they will try to pop as many balloons as possible. Each person whose balloon is popped is out and must sit down. The last player with an unpopped balloon wins for the team.

Another variation for team play requires making a center dividing line down the middle of the playing area. There also needs to be a designated goal on opposite sides of the room. One team will arrange itself by having its members spread out on their side of the playing area while the other team is selecting a raider. When both teams are ready, the raiding team sends its raider to run across to the other side of the playing area.

number: **15-50 people**

prep time: **1-5 minutes**

time required: **15-30 minutes**

playing field: **indoor/outdoor**

activity level: **high**

cleanup: **moderate**

gross factor: **none**

The raider will try to stomp on as many of the opposing team's balloons as he or she can, while the opposition will try to stomp on the raider's balloon. Anyone whose balloon was popped is out of the game. If the raider makes it to the designated goal on the other side of the playing area without losing his or her balloon, he or she is safe and can either stay there or walk back to his or her team without being accosted. If the raider's balloon is popped, then he or she is out of play and sits down. The first team to lose all of its balloons is the loser.

other variations

- Guys vs. girls
- Adults vs. students
- Play this in total darkness or with a strobe light on

2

backpack junk contest

Preparation

The week before this activity, tell the students to bring to the next meeting their backpacks filled with silly, wacky, stupid stuff. Before the meeting, create a list of just about anything a teenager might have in his or her backpack. Your list may include things such as:

- ticket stubs
- collector cards
- empty lunch sack
- one dirty sock
- pocket Bible
- fast-food wrapper
- guitar pick
- lip balm
- empty candy or snack wrapper
- detention slip
- soda cap
- comic book
- hairbrush

how to play

The game is simple: Ask for items you suspect the students might have in their backpacks. Give prizes to those who show the object mentioned, or give points to those who show the objects first. Give a prize to the one who has the most points at the end of the game.

variation

This could be turned into a race if you have access to a gymnasium. Line students up along one wall and have them place their backpacks against

number: **15-50 people**

prep time: **5-10 minutes**

time required: **15-30 minutes**

playing field: **indoor/outdoor**

activity level: **high**

cleanup: **slight**

gross factor: **slight**

the opposite wall. After you give the instruction to find a certain object, they must race to their backpacks to find the item, and then back to you to prove they have the item. You can finish with the group voting for the most unusual, the grossest, the most imaginative, the dirtiest, the smelliest (and so forth) backpacks.

3

banana mania

You can do a lot with decorations to add fun and excitement to this game, such as hanging up plastic or cardboard bananas at the door, running yellow streamers everywhere, playing banana music—"Day-o!", "Yes, We Have No Bananas"—and making an enormous banana split using a new rain gutter for the "dish."

materials needed

Lots and lots of bananas
Several varieties of ice cream
Several kinds of ice cream toppings
Banana decorations, music, yellow crepe paper streamers
A length of new rain gutter lined with plastic wrap
Plastic spoons
Several large plastic bowls
Strips of cloth for tying hands together

the games

Set up an obstacle course using chairs, cones or whatever else. If the event is being held outdoors, you can make the course over rough terrain instead. Divide group into equally numbered teams. Each team should give themselves a banana-related name—The Peels, Big Yellow, and so forth.

round 1: bananapolis 500 relay

Have team members line up behind one another. The first person in each team—while doing his or her best monkey imitation—runs through an obstacle course carrying a banana, returns to his or her team and passes the banana baton to the next member who then runs through the obstacle course. Warn them to not abuse the banana!

round 2: four-legged banana race

Two members of each team peel a banana, and then each one grasps one end of the banana in his or her mouth. They must run through the obstacle

number: **15-50 people**

prep time: **60 minutes**

time required: **60 minutes**

playing field: **indoor/outdoor**

activity level: **high**

cleanup: **moderate**

gross factor: **none**

course without dropping or breaking the banana. If they do break it, they must get a new banana and start again from where they dropped the first banana. When the first pair completes the course, they run back (without the banana) and tag the hands of the next pair on their team. Each pair repeats the process. All members of each team must run the Four-Legged Banana Race at least once.

round 3: peeling contest

With hands tied behind their backs, team members must race to a pile of unpeeled bananas, select a banana using their tied-up hands, peel it completely to the satisfaction of the judge, and then deliver the banana to the team's bowl. They will return to the line where the next member's hands are tied, and then that person is sent off to peel a banana. These peeled bananas can later be used in the banana splits—as long as they don't touch the ground!

tip

This is a great event to involve parents as helpers (or even involve them in the teams). You *will need* lots of help! If you plan on making a huge banana split, ask each student to bring either an ice cream topping or a half-gallon of ice cream to the meeting. Shop around for quantities of bananas. Pray for a great sale on bananas! You'll need lots of them!

been-there-done-that circle game

materials needed

Enough chairs for everyone

how to play

Set up a circle with chairs, having one fewer chair than the number of participants. In the center of the circle, have one person stand and tell something about himself or herself (such as something he or she has done, some place he or she has been, or a favorite sport or hobby that he or she has). For example, someone could say, "I've been to the Grand Canyon." Anyone who has not been to the Grand Canyon must get up and run for another chair. The person in the middle then has the opportunity to sit down in the circle at this time. When the chairs are full, the one still standing becomes It and must tell something about himself or herself. One rule: Participants may not move to the chairs on either side of them when they are vacated. They must get up and run for another chair.

number: **15-50 people**

prep time: **5 minutes**

time required: **10-20 minutes**

playing field: **indoor/outdoor**

activity level: **high**

cleanup: **none**

gross factor: **none**

number: **10-50 people**

prep time: **30-60 minutes**

time required: **20 minutes**

playing field: **indoor**

activity level: **moderate**

cleanup: **none**

gross factor: **none**

5

Bible treasure hunt

This game is a combination of Bible study, deduction and a race to beat the other groups to the prize.

materials needed

A Bible for each team
Slips of paper for Scripture references

preparation

Use a concordance or online source to find words and Scripture references for clues to various places around your church or ministry location. To get you started, here are a few suggested locations and matching references:

Genesis 2:9	tree
Psalm 62:3	fence
Isaiah 7:11	sign
Matthew 27:10	field
Matthew 16:18	rock
Luke 22:12	the upper room
John 12:2	table
John 19:25	near the cross
Acts 17:23	altar
Revelation 3:20	door

You will need to give the first clue to all of the teams at the same time. The remaining clues will need to be hidden around the church in the various locations.

how to play

Divide students into teams. Give all of the teams the first clue. Using the Scripture clues you have prepared ahead of time, have each team go to the suggested location to receive the next clue. The first group to reach the final destination wins the event.

variation

If you only have two teams, give each team a different set of clues, but the same destination.

number: **15-100 people**

prep time: **none**

time required: **10-15 minutes**

playing field: **indoor/outdoor**

activity level: **high**

cleanup: **none**

gross factor: **none**

birdy on a perch

This is another fun game that involves the whole group.

how to play

Have all of the guys form a circle. Then have all of the girls form a circle around the guys, with one girl standing behind each guy. The guy in front of a girl is now that girl's partner. If you have an uneven number of guys and girls, you may have to have extras sit out, use leaders and parents to even it out, or divide students by age/size. Explain that the girls are going to start walking in a clockwise direction and the guys are going to walk in the opposite (counterclockwise) direction. When the leader yells, "Birdy on a perch!" the guy is to get down on all fours while his partner runs back to him and sits on his back. The last girl to sit down is out, along with her partner. This continues until there is only one pair left.

variation

You can give the game a new face by naming it something else. For example, you could call this "surfer on a board." Anything that makes it appropriate for your group!

7

booty beach ball

materials needed

Large beach ball
Volleyball net or long rope
Several bedsheets or similar covering

preparation

This can be played outside on a grass or sand volleyball court, or it can be played indoors in a large enough room to accommodate the whole group. Prepare the playing area by stringing the volleyball net or a rope across the middle of the playing area, and then drape the sheets (or similar covering) over the net or rope so that the two sides cannot see each other.

how to play

Divide the group into two teams, assigning each team to its side of the net. Have the students sit down on their "booty" (bottoms) facing the draped net. Play with the beach ball using regular volleyball rules *except* that all the players must remain sitting at all times *and* they can hit the ball as many times as they wish. Score just as a regular volleyball game. Everything else is in play (chairs, lights, walls, people, sound equipment). Have adult leaders or non-players return out-of-bounds balls so that the players can remain seated. Play until one team reaches a score of 15, and then have the teams switch sides and play again. You can also rotate in a new team to challenge the winners.

number: 15-30 people

prep time: 10 minutes

time required: 30 minutes

playing field: indoor/outdoor

activity level: high

cleanup: none

gross factor: none

23

number: **20-50 people**

prep time: **none**

time required: **20 minutes**

playing field: **indoor/outdoor**

activity level: **moderate**

cleanup: **none**

gross factor: **none**

8

carnival guessing competition

materials needed

Cheap carnival-type toys

how to play

Select two outgoing group members who will serve as barkers—the person at a circus or carnival who entices you to play a game or see a show. The barker may also guess various facts about a contestant, such as his or her weight or age. The contestant pays a price, and the barker guesses. If the barker is correct, the contestant loses. If the barker is wrong, the contestant wins a cheesy prize.

After you have chosen the barkers, ask them to leave the room and then divide the group into two teams. Each team is represented by one of the barkers, but it is important that the barkers have no clue as to who is on their team. Once the teams are selected, ask the barkers to return and have the team members line up. The barkers will now try to guess the weight (within five pounds), the month of birth (within one month either way), or the first letter of the middle name of each member.

If the barker is correct, his or her team gets a point. If the barker is wrong, the student gets to select from a box of junky, cheesy prizes. The team with the most points wins the competition.

charades relay

preparation

The following sample checklist can be adapted to suit your group. A leader who is giving the clues scores the checklist. The first team to successfully get through the list wins. As you can see, the teams need to be separated, because they will both be working on the same titles. Customize the list to fit your group.

how to play

Divide students into two or more teams and have each team select a team captain. Next, have the team captains come to the leader for the first title and instruct them that they are to enforce the normal rules of charades (such as no talking) within their team—or have adult leaders or nonparticipating students monitor the groups. At the signal from the leader, the team captains will run back to the area assigned to their group and begin to perform their charade. Each group needs to be an equal distance from its captain and in an area where they cannot see or hear the other teams. The first student to answer correctly runs to the leader for the second title. The process continues until one of the teams completes the list.

number: **10-100 people**

prep time: **15 minutes**

time required: **30-60 minutes**

playing field: **indoor/outdoor**

activity level: **moderate**

cleanup: **none**

gross factor: **none**

Sample Checklist: Charades Relay Titles

Team A	Title	Team B
☐	TV: *Lost*	☐
☐	Movie: *The Lord of the Rings*	☐
☐	Song: "I Want to Hold Your Hand"	☐
☐	Movie: *The Wizard of Oz*	☐
☐	TV: *Survivor*	☐
☐	Song: "This Land Is Your Land"	☐
☐	Book: *Green Eggs and Ham*	☐
☐	TV: *CSI*	☐
☐	Movie: *Star Wars*	☐
☐	Song: "Jesus Loves Me"	☐
☐	TV: *Looney Tunes*	☐
☐	Movie: *Spider-Man*	☐
☐	Song: "Surfin' USA"	☐
☐	Book: *Treasure Island*	☐
☐	TV: *American Idol*	☐
☐	Movie: *The Lion, the Witch and the Wardrobe*	☐
☐	Book: *The Cat in the Hat*	☐
☐	TV: *The Simpsons*	☐
☐	Movie: *Gone with the Wind*	☐
☐	Song: "Singin' in the Rain"	☐

10

the chicken and chicken hawk game

materials needed

A large outside playing area
One raw egg for all but two players
One knee-high nylon stocking for all but two players

directions

Appoint two or more students (depending on the size of your group) to be the Chicken Hawks. Everyone else is a Chicken. All of the Chickens put their eggs in the toes of their stocking and pull the stocking over their heads until the egg is resting in the center of their heads. (You will know the stocking is on correctly if the students look like bank robbers with an egg on top of their heads.)

All of the Chickens will line up at one end of the playing area while the Chicken Hawks stand in the center of the playing area. At a given signal, the Chickens run past the Chicken Hawks to the other side of the playing area, while trying to avoid having their eggs smashed by the Hawks. The Hawks are allowed to slap the eggs with their hands. A gentle hit does the trick—no need to slam the egg.

Once a Chicken has had his or her egg smashed, he or she becomes a Chicken Hawk. The last Chicken to have his or her egg smashed is declared to be the winner.

number: **10-100 people**

prep time: **5 minutes**

time required: **20-30 minutes**

playing field: **outdoor**

activity level: **high**

cleanup: **moderate**

gross factor: **disgusting!**

number: **20-30 people**

prep time: **1 minute**

time required: **15-30 minutes**

playing field: **indoor/outdoor**

activity level: **high**

cleanup: **none**

gross factor: **none**

11

circle soccer

materials needed

A large beach ball
A long rope

preparation

Blow up the beach ball.

how to play

Divide students into two teams and have them form a large circle with team members on the same side of a circle. Next, lay a rope down the center of the circle so that the team members can tell what side they are on. Remind them that just like regular soccer, they cannot use their arms or hands to touch the ball. The object of the game is for them to try to kick the beach ball past (or over) the other team. The team members can do whatever they want to try to stop it, *except* use their arms and hands. This game moves fast. Give a point each time one team manages to get the ball past the other team. The first team to get to 10 points wins.

12

clothespin connection

This is a wild and crazy game that gets the whole group involved.

materials needed

Lots of spring-type clothespins (at least two per student)

how to play

Give each student two clothespins. On the word "go," he or she is to try to clip clothespins on the clothing of anyone else in the room. Instruct the students to stop when you signal by yelling "stop," blowing a whistle or some other action.

variation

The winner is the first one to get rid of his or her clothespins, but this can be boring, as someone is likely to be pin-less in seconds. An alternate way is to have the winner be the person who has no pins when you yell "stop!" This may create numerous winners, so you could have the "losers" sit down while the winners have a playoff round.

number: **15-50 people**

prep time: **none**

time required: **5-10 minutes**

playing field: **indoor/outdoor**

activity level: **high**

cleanup: **none**

gross factor: **none**

number: **20-100 people**

prep time: **1-5 minutes**

time required: **15-30 minutes**

playing field: **indoor/outdoor**

activity level: **high**

cleanup: **none**

gross factor: **none**

13

dodgeball games

materials needed

A large, soft playground ball (the kind used in elementary schools)
Chalk, rope or string

The Games

These games can be played inside or outdoors. Many students may have played a version of Dodgeball in elementary school, and there may be different regional versions of the rules. The students will let you know!

circle dodgeball

Have the whole group form a circle. Choose about one-quarter to one-half of the students to stand inside the large circle. Now play dodgeball with the students on the outside of the circle trying to hit the students on the inside. When a student gets hit, he or she is out and joins those forming the circle. The student can still participate by trying to hit those who are left in the middle. The last student standing in the middle wins.

prison dodgeball

Draw (with a stick in the dirt or with chalk on a hard surface) a large rectangle about the size of a volleyball court with sidelines, a centerline and a backline (see the diagram on the following page). If for some reason you can't draw a court, lay rope or string down on the ground to indicate the lines, or you can use a volleyball court (without the net) or a basketball court.

Form two teams and have them stand on either side of the dividing line. The two teams will face each other and throw the ball back and forth at each other. If a student is hit with the ball, that student is out. He or she then goes behind the opposing team's back line and is allowed to catch the ball and continue to hit the opposing team members. Eventually, the game has a few students remaining on each team's side, with a few students who are "out" standing behind the back line and still able to throw at the opposing team. The team with the last player remaining in the court wins.

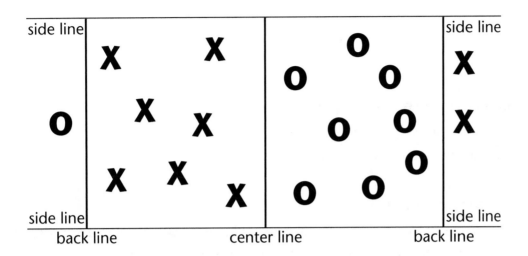

variations

- Guys vs. girls
- Adults vs. students
- Use more than one ball
- Use different types and sizes of balls
- Throw with opposite hand
- If a ball is caught before it bounces, the person who threw the ball is out instead of the person who caught it

number: **12-30 people**

prep time: **5-10 minutes**

time required: **15-30 minutes**

playing field: **indoor/outdoor**

activity level: **high**

cleanup: **none**

gross factor: **none**

14

electric fence

materials needed

A sturdy rope at least 20 feet long
Two poles, trees or other sturdy stationary objects

preparation

Tie a rope about five feet off the ground between two poles, trees or other sturdy structures. The ideal would be to use volleyball poles.

how to play

Divide the group into teams of 6 to 10 members each. The object is for everyone on the team to get over the "electric fence" without touching it. This is very similar to the kind of games seen in most ropes courses. Have the team members do this one at a time. No one is allowed to go under or around the rope or to touch the poles or the rope. If you want, you can give a team a point each time someone touches the rope. The team with the *least* number of points wins. Or you can just use this as a teamwork-building game.

variation

Assign various "handicaps" to a few of the team members—"broken limbs," a blindfold to restrict their sight, shoelaces tied together, and so on. Use any idea you can to make the challenge more interesting and fun.

15

fruit basket

materials needed

Enough chairs for everyone to be seated

how to play

Have everyone arrange his or her chair in a circle facing the middle. Have one student sit on a chair in the middle of the circle. Give everyone a name of a fruit, using only four fruits (for example, bananas, apples, oranges and peaches). The person in the middle says, "I want to eat a [name of one of the four fruits]." All of those fruits must then get up and run to another chair while the student who called out the fruit also tries to get a chair. The last student standing is now It. He or she sits down in the middle and calls a name of a fruit. Once in a while, the person who is It can yell "fruit basket's upset!" at which point everyone gets up and runs for another chair.

variations

- Use colors they are wearing: "I want to meet someone who is wearing something blue."
- Use animal names, Bible names, professional sports teams, and so forth.

number: **15-150 people**

prep time: **none**

time required: **10-20 minutes**

playing field: **indoor**

activity level: **high**

cleanup: **none**

gross factor: **none**

number: **15-50 people**

prep time: **1-5 minutes**

time required: **10-15 minutes**

playing field: **indoor/outdoor**

activity level: **high**

cleanup: **none**

gross factor: **none**

16

fruit relay

materials needed

Apples (or other round fruits or vegetables such as oranges, grapefruits or onions), one for each team

how to play

Divide your group into equal teams. Have each team line up one person behind the other and give the first person in each line an apple (or other fruit or vegetable). The first person will then place the apple under his or her chin and, on the word "go," pass the apple to the next person's chin without using his or her hands. This will continue all the way to the end of the line. The first line to completely pass the fruit to the end of the line wins.

tip

For a little added surprise, use ice-cold apples!

17

frustration

This is an add-on to familiar simple games such as tag and relay races.

materials needed

Have on hand things such as rope, duct tape, pantyhose, cloth strips, bricks or other heavy items to carry.

how to play

The object is to keep handicapping the game to make it more and more difficult to play. As the game is played, keep adding on rules. For example, tell students that all players have to play with their hands tied together—or with a water balloon tucked in their shirt, or that they have to hold their left foot up and hop, or whatever else you can think of. Keep adding on rules until the game becomes impossible to play!

number: **10-50 people**

prep time: **1-10 minutes**

time required: **15-20 minutes**

playing field: **indoor/outdoor**

activity level: **high**

cleanup: **slight**

gross factor: **none**

number: **15-50 people**

prep time: **30 minutes**

time required: **30 minutes**

playing field: **indoor**

activity level: **low**

cleanup: **none**

gross factor: **none**

18

get lost!

materials needed

3x5-inch index cards
Two baskets or similar containers
Approximately 2x2-inch squares of paper

preparation

On separate 3x5-inch index cards, write the names of enough different locations around your church to accommodate the number of students attending the meeting. Just about any place is valid—kitchen sink, boiler room door, pastor's study door, copy machine, men's room, pulpit, organ, and so forth. Place these cards in a basket or other container. Prepare lots of 2x2-inch slips of paper with the following notations: *L* (for left), *R* (for right), *S* (for straight) and *180* (for reverse—or you can use *REV*). Make enough cards for each player to have 5 (if in a small church), 8 (if in a larger church) or 10 (if in a really large church). Determine the number of moves it might take for students to get from their locations back to the youth room. Place these slips of paper in a second container.

how to play

On arrival, have each student draw one location slip. The location he or she selects will be his or her starting point. Then have each student draw the same number of slips of paper (5, 8 or 10 slips of paper, according to church size) and keep them in the order he or she drew them. On hearing the command, "Get lost!" the students will go to their starting locations and see where their list of directional cues has them end up.

The students should follow the directions in the order they drew them. For example, if a student drew the choir loft as his or her starting location, and the five directions were *L, L, R, 180, S*, the student would go from the choir loft in the direction of his or her choice. At the first intersecting corridor, doorway or other obstacle, the student would turn *left*, and then *left* again at the next opportunity to turn. He or she would turn *right* the next time, and then would *reverse* the next time and go *straight* the next time that he or she came to an intersecting hall or room. If steps are encountered, treat them as a hall.

tip

This is an imperfect game. Some of the directional choices will be impossible. If the students get stuck—as they often do—they may skip the card on top for the next one, putting the unused card on the bottom for the last direction. Trust the students to make the appropriate adjustments as they encounter dead ends. Some students will find they can go almost nowhere. That's part of the game. On rare occasions, someone's directions will actually lead him or her back to the meeting point. Award that person a cheap compass *after* you check their directions.

application

This game can have a significant teaching lead-in for lessons about following God's direction, or leading, in life. It points out that much of what life brings us is unexpected, or that we can make wrong turns that take us away from our goals rather than toward them.

number: **5-20 people**

prep time: **60 minutes**

time required: **15-30 minutes**

playing field: **indoor**

activity level: **low**

cleanup: **none**

gross factor: **none**

19

gurning contest

materials needed

Camera

Slide film

Slide projector and screen

preparation

This contest begins one week and concludes the following. It's a great way to build attendance and get students to come back! Provide a worthy prize (such as dinner for two or free movie passes) and tell everyone that he or she has a chance to win. During free time or after your meeting when students are hanging out, pull individuals aside and take their picture. Now, this is no ordinary picture. They are to "gurn." What is a gurn? A gurn is the weirdest, craziest, goofiest face they can make. Snap their picture using slide film, and then have the film developed during the week.

how to play

Show the slides to the whole group the next week. Have the entire group vote for the best gurner.

tip

Have the slides enlarged into poster-size pictures for the youth room. When students graduate, give them their poster as a going-away present.

20

hot streak

materials needed

3x5-inch index cards
Two stopwatches or watches

preparation

Write four words on each card. These can be four random words, or you can choose words related to a Bible study, retreat or meeting theme. Or you could use the key words in a Bible passage. Each list should have different but related words, with increasing degrees of difficulty.

how to play

Divide the group into two teams. Ask for two volunteers from each team. Give each volunteer a card with the four words written on it. Have each volunteer describe each word in turn for his or her group without using the word. Group members must try to guess what word the person is trying to describe. For example, if the first word is "bear," the volunteer might say, "It's a four-legged large furry animal that lives in the woods and it sounds like this: 'grrrr.'" The person can use body language as well as words, but he or she cannot use the word on the list or any form of it. Have adult leaders time each team. The first team to guess all four words the quickest wins!

number: **10-50 people**

prep time: **15-30 minutes**

time required: **15-30 minutes**

playing field: **indoor**

activity level: **low**

cleanup: **none**

gross factor: **none**

number: **20 people**

prep time: **10 minutes**

time required: **30 minutes**

playing field: **indoor**

activity level: **high**

cleanup: **none**

gross factor: **none**

human foosball

materials needed

A Nerf ball

One chair for each player

Two small portable hockey/soccer nets for goals, or four cones
    or four chairs

playing area

For this game, you will need a medium-sized room with four walls—the larger the group, the larger the room needed. However, stay somewhat confined. It is also important that the room be emptied of extra furniture to prevent accidents. The chairs should be arranged in the room using the same format as a foosball table:

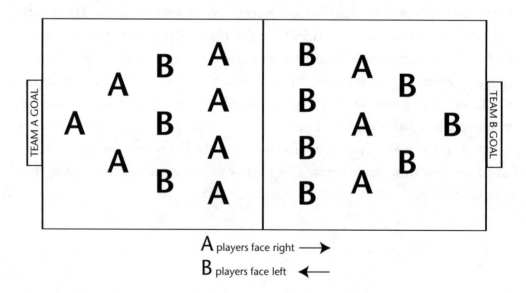

A players face right ⟶
B players face left ⟵

In foosball, the teams reflect their configurations as in a mirror, with a centerline in between to divide the team sides. Have the teams select a goalie and place him or her against the back wall to guard the goal area (Team A). The goalie's chair will stand between the two goal ends. In front of the goalie, place two defenders (Team A) and station them in front of the two goal side edges, but a good six or eight feet up from the sides. Place three members of the opposing team (Team B) on the next row facing the defenders. On the next row closest to the centerline, place four more defenders (Team A). The same setup applies for the opposing side. Goalie B, two goal defenders from B, a row of three Team A offensive players, and up on the center line a row of four more Team B players.

how to play

Play the game the same as foosball (or soccer), except that the students will sit in the chairs. They may swivel their bodies around on their chairs, but they cannot lift their bodies from the chair at anytime. They may only touch the ball with their feet. Advisors may need to be ready to retrieve balls that cannot be played.

The ball may be bounced off the walls when being passed. If it stops in an area where no players can reach it without leaving their seats, either have an advisor grab it and lob it back into the play area, or call out "up for grabs!" and designate which two of the closest students can scramble for it. These two "scramblers" cannot play it until they are once again seated.

variation

Each game will accommodate 20 players total—10 for each team. If your youth group is larger than 20, you can rotate players or whole teams or, if space allows, play two games simultaneously.

number: 15-50 people

prep time: 5 minutes

time required: 15 minutes

playing field: indoor

activity level: moderate

cleanup: none

gross factor: none

22

indoor scavenger hunt

preparation

Prepare a list of about 10 items that can be found inside the meeting room (and preferably within the team itself). Some examples include a credit card, a shiny penny, a blonde hair, a school ID, a driver's license, a note from school or a picture of the person's family.

how to play

Divide the group into teams. Stand in the middle of the room and have the teams sit in groups circled around you. Call out the name of an object to be found. The teams will then search within the group for the item, or they may send out one student to find the object within the room. The first person on a team to bring that object to the leader earns points for his or her team. The team with the most points wins.

23

kitchen olympics

preparation

Get permission to use the church kitchen. If permission is not granted, you could let the groups choose from a table of items that you have gathered from the kitchen or other source. Provide a wide variety of objects so that each team has a choice of items.

how to play

At the beginning of the meeting, divide students into groups representing countries. They may choose from a list of currently existing countries or invent a country of their own. Their task is to develop a Kitchen Olympic event that they will teach, lead and compete in. Each event needs to include some item found in the kitchen, whether a utensil, food item or whatever. (If food is available for their selection, either play outside or cover the floors of the meeting room with plastic.) The challenge is for each country team to introduce and teach its event and then have all of the teams compete against one another. The adult advisors will be the judges. Award prizes, ribbons or medals for winners, or announce that everyone is a winner and serve a dessert or other treat.

event suggestions

- Javelin throw for distance (using toothpicks or strands of spaghetti)
- Egg tossing (either how far or who can toss back and forth without breaking it)
- Find the penny in the bowl of flour (using only one hand, reach into the flour and try to grab the hidden penny, one chance per contestant)
- Soup-can bowling (roll soup cans to knock down "pins"—paper cups)
- Marshmallow stuffing (score most marshmallows held in mouth at one time)

number: **15-50 people**

prep time: **10-15 minutes**

time required: **30-60 minutes**

playing field: **indoor/outdoor**

activity level: **high**

cleanup: **moderate**

gross factor: **slight**

number: **15-50 people**

prep time: **10-15 minutes**

time required: **15-30 minutes**

playing field: **indoor/outdoor**

activity level: **high**

cleanup: **slight**

gross factor: **moderate**

24

kool-aid relay

materials needed

Several packages of the same flavor *unsweetened* Kool-Aid
Enough straws for each player to have one
Plastic drinking glasses, two for each team
One or two long tables (depending on the number of teams)

preparation

Prepare a pitcher of Kool-Aid using several packages instead of one and no sugar so that the mixture is super-strong and super-sour. Set up a table or tables at the front of the playing area. The fun part of this game is that the Kool-Aid is super strong (one recipe made with several packages) and un-sweetened. The students will think that they are going to drink this sweet liquid and get quite a shock when they taste this super-duper bitter, tart and tangy mixture!

how to play

Divide the group into 3 to 6 teams (depending on the size of your group) and have them line up one team member behind the other. Set a large glass (one for each team) filled with Kool-Aid on the tables 50 or so feet away from where the teams are lined up. Also, set an empty glass next to each filled glass. Give each member on each team a straw. The object of this game is for students, one at a time, to run to the glass with the Kool-Aid, sip some of the Kool-Aid through the straw, and then spit it back into the empty glass. The team that puts the greatest amount of Kool-Aid into the glass within a certain amount of time wins. Or, after everyone has had one turn, determine the winner by which team has the most Kool-Aid in its glass.

variation

Give the students a paper cup and straw of their own and have them race to see who is the first to transfer their Kool-Aid into another paper cup.

25

long travel games

materials needed

License Plate Scrabble: 3x5-inch index cards, hundreds of small square slips of paper, two rolls of masking or transparent tape, felt-tip pens

Stupid Sign Spotting Contest: paper, pens or pencils

Travel Scavenger Hunt: Photocopies of grid page (see page 48), pens or pencils

the games

The following games are lifesavers on longer trips when the fun of riding in a van or bus begins to wear off. The games can be adapted for use on a large bus, but are explained here for use in large 12- to 15-passenger vans.

license plate scrabble

On several of the square slips of paper, write individual letters to provide "supply letters" for the teams to draw from, but leave most of the slips blank. For supply letters, provide several with the vowels written on them and several with the most commonly used consonants. A regular Scrabble game can give you guidelines.

Many, if not most, states have letters on the license plates for passenger cars. In this game, you divide the passengers into two even teams, the front seats versus the back seats. Give each team several 3x5-inch index cards. Each team has three kinds of workers: the Spotters, who locate and call out the letters on car plates; the Scribes, who jot the letters of plates onto slips of paper; and the Spellers, who take the letters written on the slips and then create words out of the letters using the collected letters and the "supply letters" that they draw at the beginning of the game.

The game proceeds as follows. Each team draws one letter per person on his or her team. So, if there are six students per team, each team receives six letters. This is their supply. The supply is given to the Spellers who may wish to tape them on a seat for easy viewing. The Scribes (one or two are needed) are supplied with lots of slips of paper and a felt-tip pen. The Spotters need to be located next to a window where they can easily see the passing traffic.

number: **12-15 people**

prep time: **varies**

time required: **45 minutes**

playing field: **in a van**

activity level: **low**

cleanup: **none to slight**

gross factor: **none**

As a car comes into view, a Spotter calls out the letters seen on the license plate to the team Scribe. The Scribe records the letters on slips of paper and hands them to the Speller. The Spellers must then use the letters, plus up to two letters from their supply, to create words. They must use all of the available letters and no more than two additional letters. They may rearrange the letters in any way they choose, but they have to create complete words. The words are then written on the index cards.

Once a supply letter is used, it cannot be used again. When a team has used its entire stock of supply letters, it may draw six more. The game is scored by counting the most words each team creates.

predictions competition

Before a long trip, challenge the students to establish a number of predictions of happenings that will probably occur on the trip. Choose several things that can be predicted and let the students each have one guess for each prediction. Record these guesses on a chart and assign someone to keep track of the numbers. Some sample predictions include the following:

- Time of arrival at destination
- Length of the trip, in minutes
- Number of miles traveled
- Total number of gas fill-ups needed
- Total number of restroom stops
- First person to complain
- Who will get car sick
- First person to fall asleep
- First thing to be spilled
- Number of traffic jams

Other suggested predictions can be to guess what type of gas station will be the tenth one passed on the trip or which fast-food restaurant will be the twenty-first passed, and so on. Have your recorder write down the statistics as they occur. Give points for each correct guess. The highest score wins. These need to be confined to highway driving for easy tabulating—trying to keep track in a business district is pretty frustrating.

stupid sign spotting contest

Challenge the students to keep track of ridiculously worded signs along the way. Misspellings, bizarre claims or ads, announcements and the like are all fair game. Have students write down what they see so that they can share them later. Or have a group scribe record everyone's sightings, and then have him or her read the collection at the end of the day or at the end of the trip. Have students vote for the stupidest or funniest. (Incidentally, these signs can become trip slogans in no time.)

travel scavenger hunt

Since the invention of cars, games have been played using car makes or models as symbols. In the 1960s, VW Bugs were known as "punch buggies" or "slug-bugs" because the person spotting a VW and calling out its name had permission to give a good-natured punch in the arm to another person as a reward. Similar recognition penalties were linked to other cars as well, such as "Corvair, pull your hair." Today, there is the potential for a world of new innovations surrounding names or nicknames of various vehicles on the road.

Using the following list, prepare a grid sheet similar to the sample given on page 48:

- Winks—cars with broken or burned-out brake or rear lights
- Popeyes—cars with one headlight burned out
- Police cars
- Ambulances
- Tow trucks
- Breakdowns
- Trucks that sound their air horns
- Cars with ski or bike racks
- Junkers

Travel Scavenger Hunts can be informal or formal. The informal game is when the spotted car is linked to some phrase or behavior that is then acted out. However, the whole thing can become a more formal competition if you plan ahead and prepare a grid on a sheet of paper for keeping records.

When the game becomes boring, call a break until an agreed-upon time, and then resume. When a vehicle is spotted, it should be called out and identified. The first caller gets the point. The person with the most points accumulated at the end of the trip wins.

tip

For travel game winners, have prizes or awards that reflect the trip. Gather trip memorabilia such as maps, car trash bags, restaurant napkins, change found in the vehicle, car cups, toll or gasoline receipts, pebbles, shells, seeds—anything that can be collected along the way.

Sample Grid

Winks	Popeyes	Police Cars
Tow Trucks	Breakdowns	Air Horn Blasts
Ambulances	Ski or Bike Racks	Junkers

26

magazine find

materials needed

Four identical magazines

preparation

Scan the magazines ahead of time and choose about 10 items that the teams will later have to find in the magazine. Make a list of specific pictures, headlines, advertisements, and so forth. Jot down the page numbers in case you stump your students and you need to show that the item is really there.

how to play

Divide the group into four teams and have each group gather around a magazine. Call out the items one at a time. When a team finds the item called, they must rip it out and bring it to you or another designated leader. The first team to do so receives 50 points. The team that gets the most points wins!

alternate ending

At the conclusion of the Magazine Find, hand out pencils with erasers. Have each group use the erasers to create bizarre mutants by eliminating the eyes, lips or other features of people pictured in the magazine—and then retouching them with the pencils. Lots of fun!

number: **15-50 people**

prep time: **10 minutes**

time required: **15-30 minutes**

playing field: **indoor**

activity level: **low**

cleanup: **slight**

gross factor: **none**

number: **15-50 people**

prep time: **30-60 minutes**

time required: **30-60 minutes**

playing field: **indoor**

activity level: **moderate**

cleanup: **slight**

gross factor: **none**

27

mirror maze challenge

materials needed

Two large mirrors
Chairs and/or large pieces of cardboard

preparation

Use large hand mirrors or prepare one-foot square mirror tiles by applying tape around the edges (to avoid cuts). Set up a maze using folding chairs and/or cardboard, or whatever you can find to make the dividers. To avoid injuries, the maze corridors should be wide enough for two people to pass one another.

how to play

The object of the game is for the person to walk through the maze by looking into a mirror that is held out perpendicular to his or her forehead, just above the eyebrows. The reflecting surface points downward toward the feet. To maneuver, the player has to look up into the mirror to see where he or she is walking.

Divide students into teams, or you can use this as a challenge between two group members. Two students will try to navigate through the maze at the same time. If you have more than two teams, you can time each person. The one with the best time wins.

Scoring is kept by giving a point for each time a participant touches the chairs or other barricades. The object is to get the lowest number of points. Also, give points if the participant looks around and does not use the mirror continually as the viewing point. You can also keep track of the time it takes to move through the maze. Award the team with the fastest time and with the least amount of points.

28

nickname spud

Spud, that longtime staple of youth group ball games, can be adapted in a hilarious way by assigning each teenager a nickname before the game instead of the usual number.

materials needed

Several sheets of poster board or newsprint (or two portable whiteboards)
One large rubber playground ball
Nametags (or slips of paper cut the size of name tags)

preparation

Make a list of a number of nicknames equal to the number of players. Write the names in big letters on large sheets of posterboard or newsprint (or on at least two portable whiteboards) and display them around the playing area so that the players can easily see them.

how to play

As players arrive, give each person a nickname on a nametag or slip of paper. Instruct players to keep their tags in their pockets for future reference. Some will have trouble remembering the name, as they will be new to them, and they might have to refer to their nametags to remind themselves.

Have students play Spud by calling the nicknames from the posters or white boards. Have everyone bunched together in the playing area and select one person to be It. The person who is It is given the ball, and then calls a nickname as he or she throws the ball into the air. While the ball is in the air, everyone will run away from It. The person whose nickname is called is now It, and he or she has to catch or pick up the ball.

When the new It has the ball, he or she will yell, "Spud!" When Spud is called, the participants must immediately stop where they are. The person who is It may then take three steps toward any player and throw the ball to try to hit that player. If the ball is caught by the player, or if it misses the player completely, the person who is It remains It. If the player is hit by the

number: **15-50 people**

prep time: **15-30 minutes**

time required: **20 minutes**

playing field: **outdoor**

activity level: **high**

cleanup: **none**

gross factor: **none**

51

ball and it bounces off him or her, then the player becomes the new It. The game continues in this way.

There is no winner in this game. Just play for a certain amount of time or until students begin to get bored.

variation

The person holding the ball calls an identifying characteristic of the particular player he or she wants to be It. For example, if Tom wants to call Janice, he must call her by shouting something about her that everyone knows. Maybe it's the color of her T-shirt, the model of her car, her shoe brand, her favorite activity, an instrument she plays, whatever. The person must think of an identifying characteristic that everyone will recognize—it will cause confusion if the same characteristic is shared by others.

29

pantyhose event

This requires lots of pantyhose. You could ask church members to donate old pantyhose for these activities. What a great way to encourage recycling!

materials needed

LOTS of pantyhose
Several pairs of mittens (one pair for each team)
Tennis balls—two per team
Several water balloons

the games

Divide the whole group into equal teams of five to eight members per team. Be sure you have enough materials to allow full participation for the number of teams you have formed. Some of the games require only one representative from each team, while others require participation of every team member. (These games are great as part of an all-nighter or retreat.)

pantyhose putt

Divide each team in half and line up one-half of each team on one side of the playing area and the other half on the other side. Have the first person in each half face the other, with the other team members lined up behind them. Each team is then given a pair of pantyhose with a tennis ball in the toe of one of the legs. Each relay participant is to tie the empty leg of the pantyhose around his or her waist so that the tennis ball hangs behind their backs and between his or her legs.

The object is for participants to swing the tennis ball in the pantyhose leg back and forth to "putt" (hit) a second tennis ball along the ground across the playing area. Then a switch is made with the next player, who ties the pantyhose around his or her waist and putts the tennis ball on the ground back to the third player. This continues until each member of each team has had a turn.

Think of the putt as similar to the croquet putt where the mallet is sometimes swung between the legs, only the participants do not use their

number: **10-50 people**

prep time: **20 minutes**

time required: **45-60 minutes**

playing field: **indoor/outdoor**

activity level: **high**

cleanup: **slight**

gross factor: **none**

53

hands. A flat, hard surface makes the best playing field. This works well inside or on a parking lot. This is a challenging game; it could even be called difficult, but it is a blast to play and even more fun to watch.

pantyhose with mittens

Have each team choose a player to represent its team. Give each player a pair of mittens and a pair of pantyhose. The object is for the player to put the pantyhose on the quickest over his or her shoes, pants and clothes, with the mittens covering the hands. This could also be done in the form of a relay by having each team member race to put the pantyhose on and take them off, until every member has put on and taken off the pantyhose.

samurai water balloon fight

Choose one participant from each team. For each team, prepare a pair of pantyhose with a water balloon in one of the legs. Each participant then puts the elastic waist of a pair of pantyhose on his or her head. At your signal, play begins as students swing the balloons around their heads and attempt to break them against the bodies of their opponents. Play continues until all water balloons are broken. The driest person wins for his or her team.

three-legged pantyhose race

Have students remove their shoes for ease in putting the pantyhose on and off. Two people on each team will then put on a pair of pantyhose, each using one of the available legs, creating a three-legged situation. When everyone is properly garbed, have a three-legged race, or a three-legged relay race, between the teams. To make the race even more interesting, create an obstacle course for participants to race through.

30

paper plane
puzzle contest

materials needed

Four easy puzzles consisting of 35 to 50 pieces

Lots of 8.5x11-inch scratch paper

Four different colors of felt-tip pens

Four sheets of different colored construction paper—the same colors as the felt-tip pens

Transparent or masking tape

Four containers (the bottoms of the puzzle boxes work fine)

preparation

It's important that the four puzzles be very different, but that they have the same size and number of pieces. Don't get really large puzzles or any that are too small. Open each of the puzzle boxes. Using a different color of felt-tip pen for each puzzle, mark each piece on the back with a large spot. Mark all pieces of the first puzzle with one color, the second puzzle with another, and so on until each piece in each puzzle is marked. Divide the number of puzzle pieces into fourths and put one-quarter of each puzzle into each of the four containers. Each container will hold one quarter of each of the puzzles. Each will contain enough pieces to make one puzzle. Mark each container using one of the four colors that you used to mark the backs of the pieces. Tape one of each of the four sheets of colored construction paper corresponding to the puzzles to a different corner of the room.

how to play

When the students arrive, divide them into four teams of approximately equal size. Assign one of the four colors to each team (for instance, there might be a Red Team, a Green Team, a Blue Team and an Orange Team). Give each team the puzzle container that is marked with its color and then have the teams find the corner of the meeting room that has their color of

number: **12-32 people**

prep time: **45 minutes**

time required: **30 minutes**

playing field: **indoor/outdoor**

activity level: **moderate**

cleanup: **slight**

gross factor: **none**

55

paper attached to the wall. Each team will also need to be given a large stack of 8.5x11-inch paper.

Give the following directions: "This contest requires your team to successfully put together a puzzle. However, you only have one quarter of your puzzle in your container. The other teams around the room each have one quarter of your puzzle. So, the object is to get your puzzle pieces from the other groups and to get their pieces to them, as well. However, you may not simply walk over and deliver the pieces. Instead, you have to build paper planes and fly the pieces to its home group. The first team to successfully build their puzzle wins."

It is wise to assign an adult leader to each group to ensure that they do fly the pieces to their destinations. Also, one or two adults will be needed to patrol the center of the room for planes and pieces that do not make it to their destinations. These can be returned to any of the groups, equally distributing them, to groups other than their color destination for "reflying." The first team to put together its puzzle completely (and to have "flown" all the other puzzle pieces to the other teams) is the winner.

31

ping-pong launch

materials needed

Lots of ping-pong balls
Lots of plastic spoons
One empty two-liter soda bottle for each team

preparation

Cut the neck off the two-liter soda bottles.

how to play

The object of the game is for each team to try to launch ping-pong balls across the room and into their soda bottles. Divide the group into teams, making sure you have enough soda bottles so that each team has its own. Line bottles up against a wall and then line the teams up a set distance away from their bottles. (You may want to experiment with the distance before playing the game.)

Give the players on each team a ping-pong ball and a plastic spoon. Have them hold the spoon with the handle pointing away from them and toward the bottle. Then have them place the ping-pong balls in their spoons and, while holding the spoon handles in one hand, pull back the top of their spoons and the balls with the other hand (as one would a catapult). They will then release the tops of the spoons (while continuing to hold the handles) and the balls, launching them in an attempt to drop it into the soda bottle. If they hit the shot, the ping-pong ball drops through.

This can be played with everyone on the team shooting at once, or by lining the students up and having everyone shoot at once. When all of the ping-pong balls have been launched, collect each team's bottle and count the number of "bull's-eyes" each team got.

number: **10-30 people**

prep time: **10-20 minutes**

time required: **5-10 minutes**

playing field: **indoor**

activity level: **moderate**

cleanup: **slight**

gross factor: **none**

number: **15-50 people**

prep time: **30 minutes**

time required: **15 minutes**

playing field: **indoor**

activity level: **low**

cleanup: **none**

gross factor: **none**

32

pin the tail on the bear

The title of this game makes it sound like "Pin the Tail on the Donkey"— and it is! When was the last time your grown-up high school students played pin the tail on anything?

materials needed

One sheet of poster board
Several sheets of brown construction paper
Scissors
Pins, tacks or transparent tape
A blindfold

preparation

Draw a huge bear on the sheet of poster board—without a tail, of course! Make several copies of a tail on the brown construction paper and cut them out (students can do this for you). Attach the bear poster to a bulletin board (if you use pins or tacks to attach the tails) or wall (use tape for attaching the tails).

how to play

Give each player a tail with a pin, tack or tape. The first player is blindfolded, turned around a couple of times, and then pointed toward the poster. Instruct him or her to walk toward the poster with the tail in his or her outstretched hand. Don't let the player use his or her empty hand to feel along the wall. The player must walk straight ahead and stick the tail where it first touches the wall. The person who pins the tail closest to the bear wins.

33

recycling sculptures

This is more of an activity, but it also has a competition element that makes it a fun group event. It will take about an hour and a half to complete. This could also be a great activity for an all-nighter or retreat.

several weeks before

For several weeks before the event, solicit students and the congregation to bring in lots of recyclable materials such as aluminum cans, plastic bottles, cereal and oatmeal boxes, newspapers, cardboard or Styrofoam packing materials and meat trays. Collect these in large plastic trash bags.

materials needed

Recycled materials
Several Bibles
Several rolls of masking/duct tape
Utility knives and scissors
String
Wire
Heavy-duty glue and/or hot glue guns
And various other fasteners

preparation

On the day of the event, dump out the contents of all the bags together, creating one big heap (the middle of a parking lot works great). If you are using a large room—and you'll need a large room if you do this inside—be sure to put down a tarp or sheet of plastic in case the containers were not properly rinsed out. You don't want soda stains on the carpet!

how to play

When the students gather, divide them into teams of approximately five to eight members each. The teams are then assigned with the task of creating the most understandable interpretation of a Bible story, parable or

number: 10-100 people

prep time: 15 minutes

time required: 60-90 minutes

playing field: indoor/outdoor

activity level: moderate

cleanup: moderate

gross factor: slight

Bible verse. They could select their own (but they must keep it to themselves), or you could prepare some on small slips of paper ahead of time for them to draw from.

After choosing their story or passage, have each team gather supplies, spread out (around the large area or in separate rooms or designated outdoor areas) and begin to create. Give each team a time limit to complete their sculptures. After the time is up, have each team bring their sculpture back to the main meeting area. Have the other teams guess each team's story or Scripture passage.

Don't award a prize for the best or most realistic sculpture—let them stand on their own merit. Congratulate the students on their team efforts, not on the final project. Clean up by hauling the whole mess to the recycle center or to the trash bins, and then reward the whole group with an edible treat.

variation

If you really want to give out awards, give an award to each team, such as Most Imaginative, Best Use of Supplies, Most Difficult, Best Choice of Scripture, Largest, Smallest, Most Likely to Operate on Its Own, and so forth.

34

seated hide 'n' seek

materials needed

A chair
A blindfold
Small slips of paper
A black felt-tip pen
A metal pie pan
An empty soda bottle
A sign designating north

preparation

Play this version of Hide 'n' Seek in a park or other outdoor, wooded area with lots of natural cover. You will need a chair, a blindfold and a container with many slips of paper on which numerous step amounts are written (for instance, "1 step," "2 steps," "3 steps," and so on up to 10). Make a spinner by drawing lines of the eight compass directions on a round metal pie pan. Use a soda bottle as your spinner. You will also need to designate where north is in the playing area.

how to play

Set a chair in the middle of the wooded play area. Tell the students that the person in the chair will be It. He or she will be blindfolded. As It is counting to 100, the students will scurry off and hide in all directions around the area. Designate what distance (in steps) is the limit for the game.

After everyone has hidden and It reaches 100, remove the blindfold. Have It spin for the direction and then draw a step card from the container. Replace the blindfold and lead It in the direction of the spin, counting out the number of steps that was on the slip of paper he or she drew from the container. Make sure that It does not walk into trees or trip over things. If It's steps are obstructed by a tree or other obstacle, you will need to lead It around the tree and continue in the correct direction.

number: **15-50 people**

prep time: **20 minutes**

time required: **30-60 minutes**

playing field: **outdoor**

activity level: **moderate**

cleanup: **none**

gross factor: **none**

On reaching the point that the number of steps takes It, he or she removes the blindfold and "catches" the first person that he or she sees. This person is now It. If no one is in sight, It should spin again, draw another slip of paper and be blindfolded again.

tip

It's important that those who are hiding do not move around or change hiding places. Once they hide, they have to stay put. Some students might hide in front of a tree, assuming that It will walk beyond them and the tree will then become cover. Others might hide behind a tree and be unhidden as It walks past them. The students should be instructed to be partially in sight. Some will want to cover themselves with leaves or lie down in low spots or under bushes. Make a rule that they can only get down as low as sitting or kneeling. The game is no fun if It cannot see anyone to call out.

variations

- Continue play from the point of the first "find," blindfolding the one just caught and spinning from that point, walking the number of steps on the slip of paper from that point. If this option is used, a second assistant will be needed to move the chair, compass and steps container to the point of play.
- *Always* return to the original point, calling "all in free" and then starting over with the first one caught now becoming It.
- Play elimination and allow It to call out all of the people he or she sees from the destination point. Everyone else remains hidden. The first one found becomes It, returns to the chair, takes his or her turn and eliminates more from the new area of play that the designated steps and direction take him or her.

35

servant scavenger hunt

This activity is a wonderful way to promote Christian service while letting your community know that your group is active and visible. In this scavenger hunt, small groups of four to five students go into the community or to the homes and businesses of the church members to do service activities for points. At the end of the hunt, they return to the church and share their experiences.

materials

Score sheets (see next page)
Pens or pencils

preparation

Prepare a sheet similar to the sample score sheet on page 64. Make enough copies for each team to have a copy. Also, give each team a pen for gathering the signatures. Assign one adult to each team of students.

how to play

The time limit for the hunt is 1 hour, 30 minutes. Teams may not do more than two projects at one home or business. In addition, they are not allowed to take any money for the work they do—this is to be a service project for the community (or church family). At the end of the time limit, the team that has the most points is declared the winner. Close with a prayer circle thanking God that your group is located in a town that can be influenced by simple acts of love.

number: **10-100 people**

prep time: **15 minutes**

time required: **90 minutes**

playing field: **outdoor**

activity level: **high**

cleanup: **none**

gross factor: **none**

Servant Scavenger Hunt Record Sheet

Project	Point Value	Signature of Recipient
1. Mow one lawn	1,000	_____
2. Sweep three driveways	200 each	_____
3. Empty four wastebaskets	100 each	_____
4. Wash one car	500	_____
5. Sweep one garage	350	_____
6. Vacuum one living room	300	_____
7. Change one light bulb	100	_____
8. Dust the living room furniture	200	_____
9. Water two plants	250	_____
10. Vacuum the inside of one car	300	_____
11. Walk a dog around the block	400	_____
12. Clean a mirror	200	_____
13. Play ball with some kids	500	_____

Total points earned _____

Time your group returned _____

Checked by _____

36

shoe relay

The more students you have for this relay, the better!

preparation

Have everyone take off his or her shoes and throw them into a pile in the middle of the playing area. Have a leader mix up the pile of shoes.

how to play

Divide the group into equal teams of four to six members. Have each person line up in his or her team facing the pile of shoes. When you give the signal to go, the first members on each team run to the pile of shoes. Each person finds his or her own shoes, puts them on, ties them and then returns to his or her team. Then the next team member runs to the pile, finds his or her own shoes and puts them on. This continues until each team member has found and put on his or her shoes. The first team that is finished wins.

variation

Form two teams. Have players loosen their shoes (but continue to wear them) and lie on their backs in a line. The object is to be the first team to pass all shoes from one end of the line to the other and then back to the owner. The owner must then put the shoe back on. Players may not use their hands; shoes must be removed and moved along the line by foot power alone. Any shoe that falls to the ground is returned to the owner by the leader, and the owner must then pass the shoe down the line again. More than one shoe may be passed at a time.

number: **15-50 people**

prep time: **none**

time required: **10-20 minutes**

playing field: **indoor/outdoor**

activity level: **high**

cleanup: **none**

gross factor: **slight**

number: **10-100 people**

prep time: **10 minutes**

time required: **30-40 minutes**

playing field: **outdoor**

activity level: **moderate**

cleanup: **slight**

gross factor: **slight**

37

signs of nature scavenger hunt

This game can be played close to home or at a picnic, retreat, campout or church camp.

materials needed

A grocery bag for each team
Pens or pencils
Paper

how to play

Divide students into groups of six to eight members. Assign an adult to each group. Give each group a pen or pencil, paper and a grocery bag. The object of the game is for each team to collect or record as many signs of nature as possible in a given time period. Give the players a definite time period—say 30 to 40 minutes—to complete the hunt.

Teams can collect any sign of nature—egg shells, mouse bedding, spider webs, broken seeds and nuts, abandoned nests, fallen leaves, and the like. They should record things such as animal droppings, tracks, animal sightings, and such. The group with the most accumulated sightings and physical evidence wins.

tip

If the items the participants spot are collectible, they should put the objects in their bag. If not, they must have an adult advisor note it on paper. Due to the usual high level of competitiveness among students, it is advisable that an adult go with each group to rule on what is collectible and what is not.

38

"sit down if..."

preparation

Design your own personal "Sit down if . . ." list with personal references to your group. Begin the list with more general statements and gradually get more detailed. For example, tell the students to "Sit down if . . ."

- You aren't wearing deodorant tonight.
- Your grandma's name is "Thelma."
- You were born in Alaska.
- You ate ham tonight.
- You've got a poster of a rock group in your room.
- You puked this month.
- You are wearing a red shirt.
- Anyone in this room has kissed you.

Toward the end of the game, you might have to ad lib the last few statements to eliminate the last few students.

how to play

Have everyone stand up in front of his or her chair. Tell the group that you are going to read a list beginning with the phrase "Sit down if . . ." If the phrase honestly describes the person, he or she is out of the game and must sit down. The last person left standing wins!

number: **15-100 people**

prep time: **5 minutes**

time required: **5-10 minutes**

playing field: **indoor/outdoor**

activity level: **moderate**

cleanup: **none**

gross factor: **none**

number: **15-50 people**

prep time: **none**

time required: **15 minutes**

playing field: **indoor/outdoor**

activity level: **high**

cleanup: **none**

gross factor: **none**

39

sleeping bag relay

This is a "camping" game that can be played at overnighters or youth retreats. A camping theme can also be incorporated into a lock-in (an all-nighter) or a regular youth group games and activities night.

materials needed

Sleeping bags

how to play

Take any relay race and alter it by making the students stand in their sleeping bags as they do it. For example, have them do a gunny sack race where they hop along in their sleeping bags and then back to their starting position. The students will then get out of the sleeping bag, and the next person jumps in and continues.

40

spin-the-chair name game

This game works well as a means to involve the youth group in learning the names of new students. However, don't use it too soon in the new year, because the students need to know some of the names of the newer students. Wait until a month or so into the new program year.

materials needed

A swivel chair
A red and a blue felt-tip pen

preparation

Have students form a circle. They can be sitting on the floor or in chairs. Place the swivel chair in the center of the circle. Walk around the circle and alternately mark one hand of every other student with either a red dot or a blue dot. Tell the students that the color on their hands designates which team they are on—the Red Team or the Blue Team.

how to play

Choose one student to sit in the swivel chair in the center of the circle. Have the student in the chair close his or her eyes and point straight ahead with one hand. Give him or her a good spin. When the spinning stops, have the student open his or her eyes and name the person that he or she is pointing at. If the circle is large, you may need to use a yardstick as a pointer, which can be held in one hand of the student being spun. If the identification is correct, the student in the chair trades places with the student he or she correctly named. If the identification is incorrect, he or she stays in the chair and continues to try to identify the other students until he or she is correct.

Scoring can be done in two ways. One is to make it an all-group game (this works best for smaller groups) and have the students marked off with a red or blue dot on the back of their hand for team identification.

number: **10-50 people**

prep time: **none**

time required: **15 minutes**

playing field: **indoor/outdoor**

activity level: **low**

cleanup: **none**

gross factor: **none**

The students should alternate red, blue, red, blue around the circle. Scoring is done when the student in the chair identifies the person in the circle. If the person in the chair is correct, his or her team gets the point. If he or she gives an incorrect name, the person who is incorrectly named gets to be It and sit in the chair.

variation

For a large group, have the Blue Team and the Red Team compete separately, forming separate circles with their own teammates. The Blue Team gets points for correct identifications made by the person in the chair in their circle, and the Red Team does the same. Have adult leaders keep score for each team. The team with the most points at the end of the allotted rounds is the winner.

tip

Adult leaders need to supervise the game to make sure that name leaks are not whispered. Also, don't let the students know they will be playing a name game beforehand, or they might try to memorize the names of the new students at the last minute.

41

steal the bacon plus

These are suggested variations on this well-known game.

materials needed

An object to be "stolen" (such as a block of wood or piece of cloth)

how to play

Divide your group into two teams. Have the teams line up on opposite sides of the playing area, facing each other. Give each student on one team a number, and then number the students on the other team with the same numbers. Place the object to be "stolen" in the middle of the room and call out a number. The two students who have the same number (one from each team) will race to the middle to try to grab the "bacon" and retrieve it for their respective teams. That is the traditional steal the bacon game.

variations

- Call two or three numbers at a time.

- Students can also try to tag the one who steals the "bacon" and take the "bacon" away from him or her.

- Use a candy bar as the "bacon." The victor can eat the candy bar when he or she makes it back to his or her team.

- Add on stunts. For example, when a number is called, the two students must do five push ups, touch three students in line and then steal the bacon. Other examples include buying a huge pair of underwear that they have to put on, or having the students twirl a hula hoop for five seconds before stealing the bacon.

number: **15-50 people**

prep time: **none**

time required: **15-30 minutes**

playing field: **indoor/outdoor**

activity level: **high**

cleanup: **none**

gross factor: **none**

number: **15-50 people**

prep time: **none**

time required: **15-20 minutes**

playing field: **indoor/outdoor**

activity level: **high**

cleanup: **none**

gross factor: **none**

42

tent relay

This is another "camping" type game. As with the Sleeping Bag Relay, you can incorporate a camping theme into a lock-in (an all-nighter), youth retreat or a regular youth group games and activities night.

materials needed

Two identical two- or three-person tents
Optional: A stopwatch

how to play

Divide the group into at least two teams, and then divide each team in half. The first half of each team will race to put up the tent while the second half of the team will race to take it down, delivering the disassembled and packed-away tent to a designated finish line. It's really interesting to watch the students trying to work together as a team and still do it quickly. The best part is watching them try to squeeze the tent back into its bag.

variation

If you want to have more than two teams or there is only one tent available, you can time each team—the one with the fastest time wins.

43

unroll-reroll race

materials needed

At least two rolls of toilet paper, or one for each team
Masking tape

how to play

Divide the group members into at least two teams. The teams will compete to unroll a roll of toilet paper and then reroll it. However, to make it more interesting, one team will unroll the toilet paper that the other team will reroll. The teams unroll the rolls at the same time. Tell the group members that they can go up and down floors, in and out of doors, upstairs, around columns—anywhere that is acceptable to you and within the game area. However, they may not break the roll of paper. If a roll does break, they must come to you and get a piece of masking tape to reattach the paper.

When both of the teams have completely unrolled their toilet paper (leaving the cardboard roll attached), have them each find the end of the opposing team's roll. At a signal from you, they will then begin to reroll the paper onto the cardboard roll. Of course, it is easier to unroll than to reroll.

variation

If your group is large, and if you choose to do so, you may have more than two teams compete. However, make sure a different group rolls up the roll from the one who unrolled it.

alternate ending

When the game is finished, you can play other games with the toilet paper. Let your imagination run wild . . .

- You can have a "Make a Mummy" contest by having teams see how fast they can wrap one team member in the toilet paper.

- You can tape the rolls into balls with masking tape and play a variation of basketball or volleyball.

- Or you can TP the pastor's house and yard!

number: **10-50 people**

prep time: **none**

time required: **20-30 minutes**

playing field: **indoor**

activity level: **high**

cleanup: **slight**

gross factor: **none**

number: **12-50 people**

prep time: **10 minutes**

time required: **30 minutes**

playing field: **indoor/outdoor**

activity level: **high**

cleanup: **none**

gross factor: **none**

44

volley brawl

This game is best played in the sunshine with lots of students on a sand court. However, inside under fluorescent lights in the winter works fine, too. Volley Brawl is one of those games that often become legendary as the years pass.

materials needed

Volleyball and net
Volleyball court
Bell or whistle
Whiteboard or newsprint
Felt-tip pen

preparation

Write the following rules for each round on a whiteboard or on newsprint:

1. Mixed teams, regular rules.
2. Mixed teams, girls only can make a scoring point. Guys "feed" volleyball to girls. Suspend the three-hit rule, but allow no more than five hits before attempt at scoring.
3. Girls only.
4. Guys only.
5. Mixed teams, guys only can score. Girls feed ball to guys. Suspend three-hit rule as in 2.
6. Mixed teams with backs to the net. Anyone can score.
7. Volley Brawl round in which the entire team is on the court, anyone can score. Suspend the three-hit rule.

how to play

Divide the students into two teams with an even mix of guys and girls on each team. The game is divided into 7 three-minute sessions or rounds. After three minutes of play, blow a whistle or ring a bell to indicate the start of the next round. Have the new players join the game, following the appropriate rules for the round as indicated on the whiteboard or newsprint. Give the groups 30 seconds between rounds to organize for the next round.

variations

- Stationary round, professional positioning: Students have to stay planted in the regulation positions of three rows, three to a row. No one is allowed to move her or his feet. They stay planted.

- Stationary round, any position allowable: Students have to stay planted in any place they choose. It can be four in the front, two in the rear, and three in the middle, or any configuration they wish to try. Note: In this round, you may allow them to move between points.

- Tournament play: For large groups, multiple teams can compete with playoffs between two highest scores. Competition can continue over a number of weeks.

number: **15-50 people**

prep time: **15 minutes**

time required: **30-60 minutes**

playing field: **outdoor**

activity level: **high**

cleanup: **moderate**

gross factor: **slight**

45

water wars

Just when you thought it was safe to go back in the water . . .

materials needed

Three red felt-tip pens
Three blue felt-tip pens
Several children's watercolor books
Masking tape
Lots of water balloons

preparation

Buy the children's watercolor books that have the color in the paper and all you need to do is add water to bring out the color. Divide students into two teams: Red and Blue. Give each team a secret operation base and the same number of water balloons. Each team can fill its own supply of water balloons. Then give each team three felt-tip pens (or similar objects) in the team's color for them to hide somewhere on the ministry grounds. The objective is to hide the objects in such a ways as to prevent location and capture by the other team, but the objects must be visible.

how to play

Give each team member a page from the children's watercolor book. Tape one of these watercolor pages to each player's back. When a water balloon hits the player, the page taped to his or her back will turn color. A few drops do not count as a hit; there must be a large water spot to count as a hit. When a player is hit, he or she must stop immediately until a new watercolor page can be brought by a team member to be retaped to his or her back.

Offensive players attempt to "capture" the other team's felt-tip pens and take them back to their home base. Defensive players attempt to protect their pens by throwing water balloons at the enemy team members to prevent them from bringing them back to their base. If an enemy carrying the captured pen sustains a water balloon hit, the defenders may recapture their pen and return it to home base before the enemy gets another page.

The game continues until all three of one team's markers are captured and imprisoned in the other base, or until all water balloons/watercolor pages have been used up.

number: **5-35 people**

prep time: **30 minutes**

time required: **3-5 minutes**

playing field: **indoor**

activity level: **low**

cleanup: **none**

gross factor: **none**

46

what's missing?

materials needed

Sheets of newsprint or poster board
A black felt-tip pen

preparation

Cut sheets of newsprint or posterboard into 2-inch by 18- to 24-inch long strips. Write a phrase from a familiar passage of Scripture on each strip, such as the Ten Commandments (see Exodus 20:1-17), the Lord's Prayer (see Matthew 6:9-13), the Beatitudes (see Matthew 5:3-11), the Twenty-Third Psalm, the Gifts of the Spirit (see 1 Corinthians 12:4-10) or the Fruit of the Spirit (see Galatians 5:22-23). The phrases need to be complete thoughts so that they are recognizable parts of these familiar passages. For example, the Lord's Prayer would look something like this:

Our Father in heaven

Hallowed be your name

Your kingdom come

Your will be done

On earth as it is in heaven

Give us today our daily bread

Forgive us our debts

As we also have forgiven our debtors

And lead us not into temptation

But deliver us from the evil one

how to play

The game is quick and simple. Tape all the strips for the passage, except one, on a board or wall. Have the students guess what part is missing, and then have them tell what *is* supposed to be in the missing section. You can give a score for each correct answer, or simply use this game as a transition between activities (such as between game time and Bible study time). The Lord's Prayer is the easiest one and is best to use as an example or a warm-up. Most of the other suggested passages will be a challenge. You can keep these strips and use them at various times, leaving out a different strip each time.

variation

Make two copies of a passage and mix them up. Then have two teams race to put them in order.

number: **15-50 people**

prep time: **10 minutes**

time required: **60-90 minutes**

playing field: **indoor/outdoor**

activity level: **high**

cleanup: **none**

gross factor: **none**

47

when we were young games

Psychologists tell us we must occasionally "regress in service to the ego," which is a weird way of saying that once in a while it does us good to be children again. When We Were Young Games (WWWYG) is a collection of games that your students probably haven't played since adolescence kicked in, unless they baby-sit for a career, help with children's Sunday School classes, or are a few sandwiches short of a picnic.

materials needed

Large rubber playground balls
Beanbags
Chalk
Jump ropes
Pieces of cloth for flags, blindfolds, or "hankies"
Cones for marking boundaries

the games

WWWY Games feature the original versions of childhood games such as:

Capture the Flag · Kick the Can
Duck, Duck, Goose · Marco Polo
Freeze Tag · Ring Around the Rosy
Hopscotch · Red Rover

In the event that you or your students have forgotten how to play these games, the following sections will provide a brief explanation of the rules for each game.

capture the flag

A field or other area is first divided up into two sections. The players are divided up into two teams, and then each team is given five minutes to hide a flag in their section of the field or territory. After five minutes, the teams then simply try to capture the other team's flag and bring it back to their side of the playing area. If the person is caught and tagged by the other team while he or she is in the other team's territory, that person is sent to "jail" and can only be freed if another team member grabs him or her when the opponent isn't watching. The first team to capture the opposing team's flag and bring it back to their side wins.

duck, duck, goose

Participants sit down in a circle facing each other. One person is chosen to be It and walks around the circle. As the person walks around, he or she taps the other players' heads and says either "duck" or "goose." Once the person selects someone as "goose," that person gets up and chases the person who is It around the circle. If the "goose" is able to tap the player who is It before he or she is able to sit down in the "goose's" spot, the original player remains It. Otherwise, the "goose" becomes It for the next round.

freeze tag

In this version of tag, when the person who is It touches someone, that person is "frozen" in place. He or she is not allowed to move and must stand with his or her feet apart. The only way the person can become unfrozen is if another player crawls under his or her legs. Play continues until all the players are frozen. The last person to be frozen is It for the next game.

hopscotch

Get a piece of chalk or use masking tape to create a diagram with eight numbered sections on the floor. Give each player a marker (a stone, bean bag, penny, button or whatever). The first player then stands behind the starting line and tosses his or her marker into square one. He or she hops over square 1 to square 2, and then continues hopping on to square 8. Once there, the player turns around and hops back again. When the player reaches square 2, he or she must stop to pick up the marker before hopping into square 1 and then out. A player is deemed out if the marker fails to land in the proper square, or if the player steps on a line or loses balance when picking up the marker, hops into the square where the marker is before picking it up, or puts two feet down in a single box.

kick the can

First, a can is placed in a specified location. One player, who is selected to be It, closes his or her eyes and counts to 30 while the other players hide.

The person who is It then has to run around and find everybody. Once a player is found, he or she has to race back to the starting point where the can is located and kick the can before It can tag him or her.

marco polo

This game is often played in a swimming pool, but it can also be played in a field or indoors. First, select one person to be It. He or she is blindfolded (or just closes his or her eyes), and then counts to 10. After the time is up, he or she calls out "Marco," and the players respond "Polo." The person who is It then has to locate the other players by the sound of their voice. Once he or she catches a person, that person is It.

red rover

In this game, the players form two opposing lines and face each other. One team calls out, "Red Rover, Red Rover, send [John] right over." John must then let go of his teammates' hands and attempt to break through the other team's line. If John breaks through, he chooses one person from the other team to join his team, and they both go back to the other side. If John fails to break through, he must join the opposing team. The team that manages to get all of the other players is declared the winner.

ring around the rosy

Participants stand in a circle holding hands and skip in one direction as they sing the tune "Ring around the rosy, pocket full of posy, ashes, ashes, we all fall down." At the end of the line "we all fall down," the group falls down into a heap. In some versions, the last person to fall down takes the place of another in the middle of the ring.

tip

This can be a hilarious time of playing and remembering "when we were young." Be prepared to play a couple of games of your choice, and then allow the students to suggest a list of games they remember. Let them choose a game or two from their list. Note that some students will see themselves as "too cool" to participate if you advertise the actual games in WWWYG, so don't mention what they will be doing, or some may skip the meeting. However, once they are there, you'll have little trouble getting them to play.

48

winter
water balloons

An outdoor, cold-weather water balloon fight works well on a retreat or during a daylong winter activity. Have students dress warmly, covering all parts of their body with coats, snow pants, mittens, scarves, and so forth. Make sure that this is done near the meeting place. The game will move quickly, and the students will want to get warm again, but it is a pushing-the-limits kind of goofy game that will become legend in the years to come.

materials needed

Several packages of balloons

preparation

Have the water balloons filled ahead of time. Store them in two (one for each team) large plastic trash bags or trashcans in a warm place. Don't let the water balloons freeze!

how to play

Divide students into two teams. Give them boundary lines so that they do not get too far from the building. Watch for students who may be getting too cold and limit the playing time so that students do not get hypothermia. Use good judgment and do not play this if the temperatures are too cold or the wind chill too low. It can be very safe and fun, but only if you use good judgment. Have an alternate game planned in case the weather is too cold or too windy. Serve hot drinks or food after the water balloon fight to help students warm up.

number: **15-50 people**

prep time: **20 minutes**

time required: **10 minutes**

playing field: **outdoor in winter**

activity level: **high**

cleanup: **moderate**

gross factor: **none**

number: **15-100 people**

prep time: **none**

time required: **10-20 minutes**

playing field: **outdoor**

activity level: **high**

cleanup: **none**

gross factor: **none**

49

you're all it

how to play

This game is like regular tag only *everyone* is It. Everyone runs around and tags everyone else. When a person is tagged, he or she leaves the playing area and sits down. The last person standing is the winner!

Volunteer Games

volunteer \vä-len-tir\ *n* **1** : a person who voluntarily undertakes or expresses a willingness to undertake a service.

number: **6 volunteers**

prep time: **10 minutes**

time required: **5 minutes**

playing field: **indoor/outdoor**

activity level: **low**

cleanup: **none**

gross factor: **slight**

1

apple-eating contest

materials needed

Three cored apples
String

preparation

Prior to the game, cut out the center (the core) of the three apples. Tie a three-foot string through the center and tightly around the outside of each of the three apples.

how to play

Ask for 6 volunteers and divide the volunteers into 3 teams of 2 each. One person on each team (the Holder) will hold the apple while the other person (the Eater) will attempt to eat it. Have the Eaters kneel down, and then have the Holders hold the apple at the level of the Eater's face. At your signal, the Eaters will begin eating the apples without using their hands or any part of their bodies except their mouths. The Holders may not allow the apples to touch any part of their bodies. The first one to eat his or her apple wins.

2

baby feeding

materials needed

Three or four jars of baby food
Three or four plastic spoons
Several towels
A sheet of plastic

preparation

Spread the plastic sheet on the floor of the playing area.

how to play

Have three or four pairs come forward. Have one person on each team lie down on his or her back, forming a side-by-side line on the floor. Then have the other team members lie down on their backs so that their heads are touching their partners' heads and their feet are pointing in the opposite direction. Put a towel on each player's chest to protect his or her clothing. Give one member on each team a jar of baby food and a plastic spoon. This team member is to feed his or her partner the entire jar of baby food! Because they are on their backs and really can't see each other, this becomes quite a mess! The first pair with an empty jar wins.

number: **6-8 volunteers**

prep time: **1 minute**

time required: **5 minutes**

playing field: **indoor/outdoor**

activity level: **low**

cleanup: **moderate**

gross factor: **slight**

number: **4 volunteers**

prep time: **60+ minutes**

time required: **10-20 minutes**

playing field: **indoor/outdoor**

activity level: **low**

cleanup: **slight**

gross factor: **slight**

3

balls and boxes

An all-time favorite. This game works best as one event during a time of several competitions such as a game night, lock-in or retreat.

materials needed

A makeshift table made out of a piece of plywood placed on two
    supports or made out of one or two large cardboard boxes
Eight boxes of varying sizes, to cover various sizes of sports balls
Bedsheets to cover the makeshift table
Seven different types of sports balls (tennis balls, softballs, footballs)
An aluminum pie pan
Whipped cream

preparation

This will have to be set up ahead of time and, if at all possible, in an area separate from the rest of the activities. Make a table out of plywood on two supports such as sawhorses (or use a large cardboard box such as a refrigerator box). Cut a head-sized hole in the plywood (or one long side of the cardboard box). Cover the table with bedsheets, cutting a hole to match the hole in the table. Set the eight boxes on the table, and place the seventh box over the hole you have cut through the table. Volunteer one of your popular students (someone who loves to play practical jokes is the perfect candidate) to sit under the table with his or her head sticking up through the hole and covered by the box. Under the rest of the boxes, place the various types of sports balls. When the player lifts box number seven, this person is to scream at them. This usually surprises the person, and everyone gets a good laugh.

how to play

Ask for four volunteers to come up front. Tell them that they will be timed as they one at a time lift each box and name the type of ball under it. The goal is to go through all of the boxes and name all of the balls faster than the other three. Build this up and tell them the faster they do this, the better! Have three of the volunteers leave the room so that they cannot see or hear what happens to the first participant. Then have each participant compete.

Now here's the double whammy! Clue in your last participant and let him or her know exactly what is going on. But do not let the student under the box know that you have informed that student. Give this fourth student the whipped cream pie, and when he or she lifts that seventh box (and is screamed at by the student under the box), have him or her squish a pie in the popular student's face.

number: **4 volunteers**

prep time: **30 minutes**

time required: **5 minutes**

playing field: **indoor/outdoor**

activity level: **low**

cleanup: **slight**

gross factor: **slight**

4

banana split-eating contest

materials needed

A half-gallon of ice cream

A container of whipped butter (or margarine)

Four bananas

Four bowls

Various ice cream toppings (chocolate syrup, whipped cream, nuts)

A table and four chairs

preparation

Prepare the banana splits beforehand and keep refrigerated. Prepare three normal banana splits. Prepare the fourth one using whipped butter instead of ice cream. Disguise all four with lots of whipped cream and numerous toppings. Set up the table with all four chairs on one side of the table, facing the audience.

how to play

Ask for four volunteers to come forward, and then have them sit on the chairs facing the group. Bring out the four banana splits and hand one to each person. Tell them that the objective of this game is to eat the banana splits as quickly as they can without a spoon. The first one finished wins. On the word "go," have them start. It takes a few minutes for the butter-eating person to figure out there is something wrong, because the nuts, chocolate and whipped cream disguise the taste at first.

banana-eating contest

materials needed

Three large bowls
Six to nine bananas
Three blindfolds
A table and three chairs
A sheet of plastic

preparation

Set up the table and chairs with the chairs facing the audience. Cover the table with the plastic sheet. Set the bowls on the table with two to three bananas in each bowl.

how to play

This game is hilarious if done right. Be sure to carefully choose your "volunteers"—they need to be good sports. After you have chosen three students to come up front, tell them that they are going to compete against one another in a banana-eating contest. The only trick is that they will be blindfolded. After they are blindfolded, have them sit down on the chairs. Tell them that on the count of "one-two-three-go," they are to begin peeling and eating the bananas in front of them. After they get started, secretly take the blindfolds off of two of the players and watch the third person continue the contest all alone! If the right student is chosen, this is very funny. But be careful, because it could backfire!

number: **3 volunteers**

prep time: **5 minutes**

time required: **5 minutes**

playing field: **indoor/outdoor**

activity level: **low**

cleanup: **slight**

gross factor: **slight**

number: **6 volunteers**

prep time: **5 minutes**

time required: **10 minutes**

playing field: **indoor/outdoor**

activity level: **low**

cleanup: **slight**

gross factor: **slight**

candle shoot-out

materials needed

Three candles
Three candleholders
Three squirt guns
Matches
A table

preparation

Set the table up in front of the room. Fill the squirt guns with water. Put the three candles in the candleholders and set them on the table.

how to play

Ask for six volunteers and pair them up. Have one person from each pair (the "Victim") kneel behind the table with a candle set about 18 inches in front of his or her face. The other person (the "Shooter") will then kneel on the opposite side of the table, facing his or her "other half," about five feet away from him or her. Light the candles and give the Shooter a squirt gun filled with water. On the word "go," the Shooters are to try to squirt out the lighted candle in front the Victim. Watch that the Victims do not blow out the candle. The first light out wins!

92

7

caramel apple-eating contest

materials needed

Three apples
One onion
A bag or two of caramel candies
Four Popsicle sticks
Four paper plates
A rectangular cake pan or cookie sheet
A table and four chairs

preparation

Several hours before the meeting, prepare the caramel "apples." Push a stick into each of the apples and the one onion. Melt the caramels according to the package directions. Dip the apples and the onion into the melted caramels, place them in a pan or on a cookie sheet, and place into the refrigerator to cool. Set up the table and chairs facing the group. Place each of the "apples" on a separate paper plate and set them on the table, one in front of each chair.

how to play

Ask for four volunteers for a caramel apple-eating contest. Have them each sit in a chair. Tell them that they must race to see who can eat their apples the fastest. Tell them to begin when you say "go!" It takes a few seconds, but eventually the onion-eating person figures it out.

number: **4 volunteers**

prep time: **30-60 minutes**

time required: **5 minutes**

playing field: **indoor/outdoor**

activity level: **low**

cleanup: **slight**

gross factor: **moderate**

number: **3 volunteers**

prep time: **15-20 minutes**

time required: **15 minutes**

playing field: **indoor/outdoor**

activity level: **low**

cleanup: **none**

gross factor: **none**

8

cartoon creation

materials needed

The comics pages of a newspaper
Pens or pencils
Overhead projector and transparency

preparation

Cut out a simple cartoon from your local newspaper. Enlarge it and remove the captions or speech from the balloons. Make three copies on plain paper.

how to play

Ask for three volunteers, and give each of them a paper copy of the cartoon. Give them three minutes to fill in the blanks. Tell them that the funniest one will win. After they have completed their papers, bring them up to the front and share the original caption on the cartoon strip. Then read the three captions written by the volunteers. The funniest one wins! You can have the rest of the group vote.

variation

Divide the group into teams and have them work together on the captions.

donut dunkin'

materials needed

Three donuts
Three towels or one large plastic sheet
String
Chocolate syrup
Three bowls

preparation

Tie a three-foot length of string through the hole and around the side of each of the donuts.

how to play

Ask for six volunteers, and then pair them up. Have one person in each pair lie down on a towel or plastic sheet. Give the second person in each pair a donut with the string tied around it. Have each standing partner hold the end of the string and dip the donut into a bowl of chocolate placed next to his or her partner's head. The object is for the ones lying down to eat all of the donut without using their hands. Their partners must dunk the donuts into the chocolate after each bite. The first one done wins!

number: **6 volunteers**

prep time: **10 minutes**

time required: **5-15 minutes**

playing field: **indoor/outdoor**

activity level: **low**

cleanup: **moderate**

gross factor: **slight**

number: **8 volunteers**

prep time: **15-30 minutes**

time required: **5 minutes**

playing field: **indoor/outdoor**

activity level: **low**

cleanup: **slight**

gross factor: **slight**

10

egg roulette

materials needed

Twelve eggs

A pan

Optional: Easter egg dye

preparation

The day (or several hours) before, boil 11 of the eggs, leaving 1 of the eggs uncooked. Discard any eggs that may have cracked while boiling. If you want to add some color to the activity, dye all of the eggs, including the raw egg. When the eggs are dry, return them to the carton and refrigerate until you need them.

how to play

Ask for 8 volunteers and have them come forward. Line them up side by side and tell them that they are about to play a game of egg roulette. Each of them is to pick an egg from the carton and crack it over the head of the person next to them. This continues until the raw egg is broken.

11

eggs and stockings chicken fight

materials needed

Four knee-high stockings
Four eggs
Newspapers (or cardboard rolls from paper towels, plastic wrap or
   gift wrap)

how to play

Ask for four guys to volunteer, and then assign each of them a female partner. Place a knee-high stocking over each guy's head and put a raw egg in the toe of the stocking so that the egg rests on top of their heads. Next, have the girls get up on their partners' shoulders for a chicken fight. Give each girl a section of rolled-up newspaper (or a cardboard roll). On the signal from you, the girls are to try to protect their guys while trying to break the other guys' eggs. The last team with an unbroken egg wins!

number: **8 volunteers**

prep time: **5 minutes**

time required: **5 minutes**

playing field: **outdoor**

activity level: **low**

cleanup: **slight**

gross factor: **moderate**

number: **3 volunteers**

prep time: **5-10 minutes**

time required: **5 minutes**

playing field: **indoor/outdoor**

activity level: **low**

cleanup: **slight**

gross factor: **moderate**

12

eggs-in-a-bottle

materials needed

Two dozen eggs

Three clean, empty soft drink bottles

A table and three chairs

A sheet of plastic

Sponges

Towels

preparation

Set up a table in front of the room. Place the three chairs behind the table, facing the audience. Cover the table with a sheet of plastic. Place the three bottles on the table.

how to play

Ask for three volunteers to come forward and sit down at the table facing the rest of the group. Instruct them that on the word "go," they will break the first egg and then squeeze as much of that egg into the bottle as possible. The first person to fill up the bottle wins!

tip

Have sponges and towels ready for cleanup. Also, have adult leaders prepared to thwart any ideas of an egg fight following the contest.

13

guys, gloves and pantyhose

materials needed

Three blindfolds
Three pairs of large gloves
Three pairs of pantyhose
Three chairs

how to play

Ask for three or four male volunteers. Have them sit on chairs facing the crowd and remove their shoes. Tell them that they are to reach forward and pick up the pantyhose that will be laid out on the floor in front of them, and then pull the pantyhose on over both legs all the way up to their waists. The first one to do this wins. The trick is that the volunteers are going to be blindfolded and will be wearing gloves, which will make this much harder. When they are blindfolded and in gloves, say "go." Have a camera ready!

number: **3-4 volunteers**

prep time: **5 minutes**

time required: **5-10 minutes**

playing field: **indoor/outdoor**

activity level: **low**

cleanup: **none**

gross factor: **none**

number: **3 volunteers**

prep time: **10 minutes**

time required: **5 minutes**

playing field: **indoor/outdoor**

activity level: **low**

cleanup: **slight**

gross factor: **slight**

14

ice fishing

materials needed

Two to three dozen marbles
One large tub of water, large enough for at least three large feet at a time
A large bag of ice
Three large towels
Three chairs
A sheet of plastic

preparation

About 30 to 40 minutes before doing this activity, put about two to three dozen marbles in the tub, and then fill the tub about half full with ice and water. This will give the ice time to melt and make the water especially frigid. Lay the plastic sheet on the floor and set the tub of water in the middle of it with the chairs arranged in a half circle around the tub.

how to play

Ask for three volunteers. Have them sit in the chairs facing the group, and then instruct them to take off their shoes and socks. Tell them that they are going fishing. Their task will be to use the toes of one foot to try to pull out as many marbles as they can in one minute. The one who pulls out the most marbles wins. The only trick is that the container of water is also full of ice water.

variation

Exchange the marbles for olives, pickles . . . or whatever else.

15

ketchup race

This crazy game is fun to watch because it creates a huge mess, so plan on playing this game outside, or cover the playing area with plenty of plastic!

materials needed

Nine to twelve fresh, ripe tomatoes
Three to four clean, empty soft drink bottles
Optional: A sheet of plastic (if playing this inside)

preparation

If you are not doing this outside, lay down a sheet of plastic on the floor and set the soft drink bottles on the plastic.

how to play

Ask three or four volunteers to come forward. Have the volunteers kneel down in front of a soft drink bottle, facing the crowd. Give each of them three tomatoes, and then tell them that on the word "go" they will have one minute to make as much ketchup as they can. Whoever squeezes the most tomatoes into the soft drink bottle wins.

number: **3-4 volunteers**

prep time: **5 minutes**

time required: **10 minutes**

playing field: **indoor/outdoor**

activity level: **low**

cleanup: **slight**

gross factor: **moderate**

number: **3+ volunteers**

prep time: **30 minutes**

time required: **30 minutes**

playing field: **indoor**

activity level: **low**

cleanup: **none**

gross factor: **none**

16

know-my-kid game

This game can be a powerful tool for bringing families closer together in a fun and humorous fashion. Try it! Adapt it!

preparation

During a session a week or two before an upcoming parents' meeting, give the students the survey on the following pages (or make up a survey of your own). Choose the three surveys from the students that have the most humorous or interesting answers. These will be the contestants for the "Know-My-Kid Game" that will be played during the parents' meeting. Make sure that the students you choose don't mind and that their parents are going to attend the event. (Both the students and their parents need to be good sports.)

how to play

At the parents' meeting, invite the parents of your chosen contestants to come up front. Read the questions and ask the parents for the response that they think their teenager picked. Parents receive points when they guess correctly. If you use the questions on the prepared survey, don't use every question. Select about six or eight of the best questions.

This game can be used as a lead-in for more serious discussions of communication and family harmony. For debriefing after the game, you can ask parents what they thought of the game, what one thing they would like to tell their sons or daughters about how they feel toward them, and how students and parents can build each other up as a family united in Christ.

Appropriate Scriptures to use include Romans 14:13,19; 1 Corinthians 13:1-8; Ephesians 4:25-27; 6:1-4; Colossians 2:2-3; 3:20-21; 1 Thessalonians 5:11; James 3:2-12; 4:1-3.

variation

Do this in reverse. Ask parents to fill out similar surveys and have students decide how their parents answered.

The Do-You-Know-Me Survey

Please complete as much of this survey as you feel comfortable doing. Note: Some of these answers might be shared in front of the youth group and parents. Be open and sensitive, yet honest!

1. My parents are as excited about going to church as if . . .
   A. Church was giving away free money.
   B. Church was as routine as going to work.
   C. Church was like getting a root canal.

2. In a discussion about "the birds and the bees" . . .
   A. My dad told me the facts of life.
   B. My mom told me the facts of life.
   C. I had to tell my mom and dad the facts of life.

3. My parents treat me as if . . .
   A. I'm the most important thing in their lives.
   B. I'm somewhere between irritating and annoying.
   C. Slavery is still legal and they're my masters.

4. An appropriate T-shirt for my parents would read . . .
   A. "Parent of the World's Greatest Kid"
   B. "Take My Kid—Please"
   C. "Property of the Insane Asylum"

5. My grades at school make my parents . . .
   A. Proud as can be.
   B. Loud and upset.
   C. Claim they don't know me.

6. Which type of breakfast cereal best describes your parents?
   A. Corn Flakes
   B. Grape Nuts
   C. Fruity Pebbles

7. My communication with my parents is . . .
   A. Great—we talk all the time.
   B. Okay—they hear from me at least once a day.
   C. Not so good—our last meaningful talk was when I was seven years old.

8. In your family, who is the loudest snorer? _____

9. What is your mom's favorite TV show? _____

10. What is the meanest trick a parent has ever played on you?

_____

_____

11. What holiday is the biggest deal in your family?

_____

12. What would your parents do if they won a million dollars?

_____

_____

13. Who is the best cook in your family? _____

14. What is the worst chore you have to do? _____

15. What is the neatest way a parent shows you that you are loved?

_____

16. When is your curfew? _____

17. What do you want to be?

_____

18. What is the most common way for your parents to embarrass you in front of your friends?

_____

_____

19. If you could tell your parents just one thing about how you feel about them, what would it be?

_____

_____

_____

20. If your parents could tell you one thing about how they feel about you, what would it be?

_____

_____

_____

17

lemonade-eating contest

materials needed

A box of individual sugar packets
A lemon for each participant
Large glasses of water

preparation

Cut each lemon into quarters. Fill the glasses with cold water.

how to play

Ask for three volunteers to come forward, and then have them sit in chairs facing the rest of the group. Give each volunteer two packs of sugar, a lemon (cut into quarters) and a large glass of cold water. On the word "go," they must first eat the sugar, then eat the lemon, and finally drink the water. The first one to finish the sugar, lemon and glass of water is the winner. The results are hilarious!

number: **3 volunteers**

prep time: **5 minutes**

time required: **5 minutes**

playing field: **indoor/outdoor**

activity level: **low**

cleanup: **slight**

gross factor: **moderate**

number: **6 volunteers**

prep time: **none**

time required: **5 minutes**

playing field: **indoor/outdoor**

activity level: **low**

cleanup: **slight**

gross factor: **none**

18

lipstick contest

materials needed

Three tubes of lipstick—bright red is the best

how to play

Ask for six volunteers—three guys and three girls. Pair up each guy with a girl. Have each girl hold the metal tube-part of lipstick in her mouth with the red tip facing outward. Have each guy then proceed to apply the lipstick to his mouth by moving only his mouth (with his hands held behind his back). Give the pairs one minute to apply the lipstick. You can have judges determine who put the lipstick on the best, or have the whole group vote.

19

oogie boogie

materials needed

Three large sponges
A container of water
Three chairs

how to play

Tell the group that you are going to see who is the strongest guy in the group. Have three strong guys come forward. Then choose three girls of about equal size (to one another) to come forward as well. Have the girls sit in chairs facing the crowd. Have each guy stand behind a girl and also face the crowd. On the count of three, have the guys lift the girls by their elbows and hold them up for as long as they can. When the girls are in the air, have a leader sneak a soaking wet sponge onto each of the chairs. After a moment, have the guys give in and set the girls back down. It takes a second before they realize that their seats are soaking wet!

number: **6 volunteers**

prep time: **1 minute**

time required: **5-10 minutes**

playing field: **indoor/outdoor**

activity level: **low**

cleanup: **none**

gross factor: **slight**

number: **8 volunteers**

prep time: **10-15 minutes**

time required: **15 minutes**

playing field: **indoor/outdoor**

activity level: **low**

cleanup: **heavy**

gross factor: **slight**

20

pass the pie

materials needed

One or more aluminum pie pans
One to two aerosol cans of whipped cream
A sheet of plastic
CD player or stereo

preparation

Fill one or more aluminum pie pans with whipped cream. Although you will only use one pie at a time, it is a good idea to have more than one ready to save time refilling the pan.

how to play

Ask for eight volunteers and have them line up side by side across the front of the group. Give the first person in line the pie pan filled with whipped cream. As music is played, have each person pass the pie from one person to the next. Any person holding a pie can only hold the pie for up to two seconds, and no longer. The person playing the music should be blindfolded or have his or view of the volunteers blocked so that he or she can be completely impartial. When the music stops, the person left holding the pie has the option of hitting the person on the left or right in the face with the pie. When this occurs, the one who is hit with the pie sits down. The music starts again, and the pie is passed until the music stops again. Play continues until the person left holding the pie gets to hit the only other person still standing. When the pie reaches the end of the line of eight people, have the last person pass it back the other way.

21

ping-pong bounce

materials needed

Two or more ping-pong balls
Two or more ping-pong paddles

how to play

Select two or more volunteers, or have a representative from each team come forward. The object of the competition is for the volunteers to take a ping-pong paddle and bounce a ping-pong ball up and down as many times as possible without missing the ball. The trick is that the person must hit the ball on one side of the paddle and then flip the paddle over to the other side. This can be done with both competitors bouncing their balls at the same time, or with each one doing it separately. This continues back and forth until the ball is missed. Have the whole group count the number of hits for each person out loud. The person with the most hits wins!

variations

- Guys vs. girls
- One member of one team vs. a member of another team
- One grade level vs. another grade
- Any other combination you can think of!

number: **2+ volunteers**

prep time: **5 minutes**

time required: **5 minutes**

playing field: **indoor**

activity level: **low**

cleanup: **none**

gross factor: **none**

number: **6 volunteers**

prep time: **none**

time required: **10 minutes**

playing field: **indoor/outdoor**

activity level: **low**

cleanup: **moderate**

gross factor: **none**

22

santa beards

This is a great Christmas game.

materials needed

Three cans of shaving cream
Three towels
Three chairs

how to play

Have three guys volunteer to come forward, and then ask for three girls to volunteer. Have the guys sit in the chairs. Wrap towels around their necks and chests. Give each girl a can of shaving cream. Tell the girls that they are to create the best-looking Santa beard on their partners. This is not a timed contest, so tell the girls to take their time and try to create the very best beard they can. Give them about three to four minutes to complete the beards. Have the rest of the group vote for the best beard.

23

space helmet

materials needed

Several pairs of new surgical gloves

how to play

Ask for as many volunteers as there are gloves. Give each person a surgical glove. Have each of them place their gloves over their heads and their noses (but not their mouths!). At your signal, tell them that they are to inflate the glove by blowing through their noses. The first one to blow up and pop their glove wins! The results are hilarious. Have your camera ready for this one!

number: **2+ volunteers**

prep time: **none**

time required: **5 minutes**

playing field: **indoor/outdoor**

activity level: **low**

cleanup: **none**

gross factor: **moderate**

number: **6 volunteers**

prep time: **1 minute**

time required: **5-10 minutes**

playing field: **indoor/outdoor**

activity level: **low**

cleanup: **none**

gross factor: **disgusting!**

24

stick 'em up

materials needed

A large jar of peanut butter
Three rubber spatulas
A large container of cheese ball snacks
Three plastic bags

preparation

Divide the cheese balls between the three plastic bags.

how to play

Ask for six volunteers and pair them up. Have three of the volunteers stand facing the group. Have the partners for each put smooth peanut butter all over their faces, using the rubber spatulas, and then stand about five feet away from them. Give each of the partners (the ones without the peanut butter on their faces) a bag of cheese balls. On the word "go," have them toss the cheese balls at their partners' faces and try to get the balls to stick. After one minute, the team with the most cheese balls stuck wins!

25

sticky dime

materials needed

A dime
A chair

how to play

Ask for three volunteers and have them come forward. Have two of the volunteers leave the room. Tell the remaining person that you are going to stick a dime on his or her forehead and that he or she is to contort his or her face until the dime falls off. Demonstrate this by pressing a dime firmly on his or her forehead. Time the participant, telling him or her that this is just a practice round (this usually takes a few seconds). Praise the participant for his or her success and say that now, for the real contest, he or she will be timed.

This time, instead of actually pressing the dime on the person's forehead, hide the dime and press only with your finger (it will feel the same to the person). Press hard for three or four seconds, and then remove your finger and say "go." Have the crowd encourage the student to do his or her best to get that dime off. Continue this until the person finally realizes that there is nothing on his or her forehead.

After the first person is let in on the trick, bring in the other participants one at a time and repeat the process.

number: **3 volunteers**

prep time: **none**

time required: **10 minutes**

playing field: **indoor/outdoor**

activity level: **low**

cleanup: **none**

gross factor: **none**

number: **6 volunteers**

prep time: **10 minutes**

time required: **10 minutes**

playing field: **indoor/outdoor**

activity level: **moderate**

cleanup: **slight**

gross factor: **none**

26

team skiing

materials needed

Six four-foot-long 2x4s
Duct tape

how to play

Ask for six volunteers: three guys and three girls. Pair the guys and girls and tell them that they are going to have a "ski" race against the other teams. Give each couple two of the 2x4s. Have several students help each participant tape their feet securely onto the 2x4s—both left legs on one board and both right legs on the other with one person behind the other. When this is done, each pair will have all four feet taped onto their "skis." Next, have the helpers help the couples stand up and tell them that they cannot move unless they move together. On the signal "go," they are to "ski" together around a designated course and then return to the starting point. The first pair to return wins.

27

tootsie dogs*

materials needed

Four large Tootsie Rolls
Four paper plates

how to play

Ask for four volunteers to come forward. Give the volunteers a large Tootsie Roll and ask them to begin chewing. Give the volunteers a paper plate and tell them that they have one minute to form a "Tootsie dog" in their mouths with the Tootsie Roll that they are chewing. After one minute, they are to spit the Tootsie dog onto their plates. Have adult leaders judge. The best Tootsie dog wins!

number: **4 volunteers**

prep time: **1 minute**

time required: **5 minutes**

playing field: **indoor/outdoor**

activity level: **low**

cleanup: **none**

gross factor: **disgusting!**

---

* **tootsie dog** \tut-se däg\ *n* a chewed Tootsie roll formed in the shape of something a dog would leave in the back yard.

number: **3 volunteers**

prep time: **5 minutes**

time required: **5 minutes**

playing field: **indoor/outdoor**

activity level: **moderate**

cleanup: **moderate**

gross factor: **moderate**

upside-down soda contest

materials needed

Three cans of soda pop
A large sheet of plastic

preparation

Lay the sheet of plastic on the floor where the contest will take place.

how to play

Ask for three volunteers, and have them stand in front of the group. Place a can of soda on the floor in front of them, and then tell them that they are going to have a soda-guzzling contest. This is no big deal . . . except that they must stand on their heads to do it. Have someone help them get on their heads, and then hold their feet. Once they are in place, say "go" and watch the chaos! The first one finished wins.

29

what would you do for a dollar?

This is a crazy, ongoing game that can last for weeks.

materials needed

A small plastic bowl and/or glass
Any combination of foods or liquids to mix
Several one-dollar bills

how to play

To begin with, ask students what they would do for a dollar. Ask, "Would you eat/drink this?" Then concoct a nasty mixture of foods or liquids in the bowl or glass in front of the whole group, but don't get too carried away the first week. For example, make the concoction a mixture of mayonnaise, Tabasco sauce, lemon juice, a soft drink and grape jelly. Ask for a volunteer, assuring him or her that if he or she eats/drinks this concoction, he or she will get a dollar. Do the same thing the following week. Each week, make it a little crazier, a little nastier.

tip

Have a garbage can nearby just in case.

number: **1 volunteer**

prep time: **10 minutes**

time required: **1-2 minutes**

playing field: **indoor**

activity level: **low**

cleanup: **moderate**

gross factor: **disgusting!**

number: 6 volunteers

prep time: 1 minute

time required: 5 minutes

playing field: indoor/outdoor

activity level: low

cleanup: slight

gross factor: slight

30

whistle and burp

materials needed

Crackers

Cans or paper cups of soda pop

how to play

This contest consists of three teams of two members each competing against each other. It's often best when the teams are made up of one guy and one girl. The objective is for one member from each team to eat two crackers and then, on completion, to whistle. After that team member has whistled (and the judge has heard it!), the next team member will guzzle a soft drink as quickly as possible, and then burp. The first team to achieve a burp wins.

variations

You can add to this game by adding team members and stunts that must be performed. For example, a third member would drink a glass of water and then cough; a fourth would eat a teaspoon of peanut butter and then whistle; a fifth would chew a piece of gum then blow a bubble, and so on.

ICEBREAKERS

icebreaker \ is-bra-ker \ *n* **1** : something that breaks the ice on a project or occasion; especially : MIXER. **2** : a ship equipped (as with a reinforced bow) to make and maintain a channel through ice.

Icebreakers are activities designed to bring a group together by reducing the "space" between group members. "Space" may mean physical distance between people, but more often it means emotional distance. The purpose of icebreakers is to bridge the gaps between individuals so that they can get to know one another in a lively and entertaining way.

The following icebreakers have been divided into two categories. *Crowdbreakers* are typically brief activities used at the beginning of a session to warm up the group, although they can also be longer activities that take the entire meeting time to complete. They can be adjusted to any size group and, except in a few instances, do not require a lot of prep time. *Community Builders* are used to encourage the development of ongoing relationships within the group or to fulfill a specific goal of the group. Some are brief, others are longer in duration, and one takes the entire year to do correctly.

Visitors need an opportunity to become part of the group as soon as possible, so we have chosen icebreakers that groups of any size can use. Longtime members need to know that they continue to have an important part in the group. Younger students just entering the group need some assurance that they are accepted. Crowdbreakers and Community Builders are great for accomplishing all of these goals.

Special thanks to whoever it was out there in ministryland who dreamed up these gems. To each of you originators, we tip our hats and assure you that if we knew who you were, we would have given you full credit.

crowdbreakers

crowd \kraud\ *n* **1** : a large number of persons especially when collected together : THRONG **2 a** : the great body of the people : POPULACE **b** : most of one's peers <follow the crowd>.

breaker \bra ker\ *n* **1 a** : one that breaks **b** : a machine or plant for breaking rocks or coal **c** : a device for opening a circuit; specifically : CIRCUIT BREAKER

1

american hero

It's a mystery how this fun icebreaker got its name, but it works!

how to play

First, have all of the guys get in the middle of the room or playing area and tell them to lock their arms and legs as tight as they can. The girls will then try to pull the guys apart until there is only one guy left. This wild free-for-all is a blast. Not only that, but it does just what it is supposed to do—mixes all the students together. Now switch and have the girls lock arms and legs, and the guys will try to break them apart.

number: **any size group**

prep time: **none**

time required: **5-10 minutes**

number: **any size group**

prep time: **none**

time required: **1-5 minutes**

2

anthology of holey tales

Students love to tell "tall tales"—stories that obviously did not happen, could never have happened, and likely will never happen. This crowdbreaker gives your group an opportunity to be creative and entertain one another with their stories.

materials needed

Lifesaver candies

preparation

The week before this activity, ask students to wear their holey socks to the next youth group meeting. Tell them that everyone who does will be awarded a prize.

how to play

As the group gathers for the meeting, ask the students to remove their shoes and leave them at the door. Divide them into groups of three or four, and then have the students show off their best sock holes in their small groups. Give a Lifesaver candy to each person who has a hole-in-one sock.

Next, tell the group that you have heard that some of these holes have amazing origins and that you know for a fact that the current wearers either know the story of the hole or have experienced the hole-making event themselves. Tell the small groups to share with one another the how, who, why, when, what and where of the tale of the creation of each of their sock holes. Tell the students that you are looking for wild yet nearly believable stories. Have each group select the best story for reporting to the whole group.

When this activity is completed, wave your hand in front of your nose and beg the students to put their shoes back on.

variation

Have the small groups mix and mingle bits of each member's story for a story to be told to the whole group.

122

3

bags of fun

number: **any size group**

prep time: **10-15 minutes**

time required: **10-15 minutes**

This simple icebreaker will get every student mingling with others.

materials needed

Four small slips of paper
A pen or pencil
Four paper bags, lunch-sized is fine
Four surprises to be put in the bags, your choice

preparation

Write the numbers 1, 2, 3 or 4 on four individual slips of paper, with one number on each paper. Give four students a slip of numbered paper to put in their pockets, and then plant these students within the group. Prepare four "Bags of Fun"—lunch-size bags with a prize in each bag. Staple the bags closed so that no one can peek. These prizes might be a candy bar, a gift certificate, plastic toy or an onion. Let your imagination run wild!

how to play

Have everyone stand up and walk around and mingle with other students. At a designated signal—the music stops, a whistle blows, or whatever you devise—have the planted person with the number 1 grab a nearby student, find out that person's name, and then yell "John has won the first prize." John then picks one of the four "Bags of Fun" held by an adult leader. Whatever is in that bag, John gets. Who knows? After the first person picks a prize, have the group continue mingling until all four bags are claimed.

number: **any size group**

prep time: **none**

time required: **15-20 minutes**

bogus introductions

materials needed

Paper

Pens or pencils

how to play

This is a hilarious way to introduce people to each other in a group when there are many new faces. First, divide the students into groups of two. No one is to be paired with a person who he or she knows well (it works best if they are complete strangers). Next, give each player a pencil and a piece of paper. Allow the teams to have a few minutes to say hi and tell a bit about themselves, and then give the following instructions:

> You have now gotten to know your partner better. What I want you to do now is to write an introduction for your partner—a completely bogus introduction. For example: "This is John Smith. John is currently skipping his junior and senior year at high school to lead the surgical unit at Community Hospital, where he will be the surgery trainer of new resident doctors. He is not married, believing that commitment to one woman would put all of womankind into a deep depression. So he dates a different woman every free evening. He loves to field scuba dive, especially in cornfields throughout the Midwest. His dream is to establish lisping as an acceptable language form, and his favorite food is found in the pet section of the local grocery—Kibbles and Bits.

The level of laughter will only be exceeded by the amazing creativity the students will display. Promote good introductions and tell the students not to be vicious or offensive. Have them use the paper to jot down a few notes about how they will introduce their partners. After sharing, if you have time, have students stand up and share who they really are.

clue stories

number: **any size group**

prep time: **none**

time required: **15-20 minutes**

Clue stories are easy to do, require little preparation, and get group members talking with each other.

how to play

A clue story is one in which you give the end of a mystery and have the students try to guess the events that led up to the tragedy. Participants ask questions, to which you can only answer yes, no or "makes no difference" (use this last response if the question has no bearing on the story). You can also repeat the ending if asked.

the clue stories

You can make a clue story last for a long time, or even continue the crowdbreaker at a future date if you are coldhearted enough not to reveal the truth to the hapless guessers. Or, by dropping a few hints, you can wrap up the story in a shorter time.

fred is dead

The Clue: There is a stray gunshot. In the room there is broken glass and liquid on the rug. How did Fred die?

The Story: A neighbor kid shot wide with his BB gun. The pellet came through the window and shattered the fishbowl. Fred is a fish, and he died as all fish do when they are left out of water: he suffocated.

the hanging man

The Clue: When they found the man, he was in a room locked from the inside with no furniture or windows, only a puddle of water on the floor. The man was hanged with a belt from a lamp fixture in the middle of the ceiling. How?

The Story: The man hanged himself by standing on a block of ice, which had since melted.

a winter day

The Clue: A man lies dead in his bed. There is snow outside and a glass of discolored water on the nightstand. What happened?

The Story: The man was stabbed with an icicle, which the attacker then placed in the glass. The icicle melted, leaving bloody water in the glass.

the man in the desert

The Clue: A man lies dead in the desert, facedown, and wearing a backpack. What happened?

The story: The man was skydiving, and his parachute failed to open.

tom, dick and harry

The Clue: Tom, Dick and Harry are home together one night. Due to the high crime rate in the neighborhood, the house is securely locked. Dick leaves the room for a few seconds. When he returns, he discovers that Tom is there, but Harry has disappeared. Dick knows that Harry did not have enough time to leave the house. He asks Tom where Harry went, but Tom refuses to answer. Where did Harry go?

The Story: Tom, Dick's cat, ate Harry the mouse.

comb! clean! count!

number: **any size group**

prep time: **none**

time required: **10-15 minutes**

This is a really strange competition that will truly break up a crowd.

materials needed

Lots of cheap plastic combs
Sheets of newsprint
Tables or areas of open floor space

how to play

Divide the students into groups of no more than four people per group. Give each student a comb (or he or she can use his or her own clean comb). Tell students to comb 10 strokes through their hair and then empty the comb and count the number of hairs. Give the commands, "Comb! Clean! Count!" The team that produces the most hairs within 40 total strokes wins the competition. This can be a great lead-in to a study on Samson, the woman in Luke 7:36-50 who cleaned Jesus' feet with her own hair, or other verses with references to hair. Or just do it to have fun.

number: **any size group**

prep time: **1-5 minutes**

time required: **5-10 minutes**

7

do as I do

materials needed

Small paper cups
Pitchers of water

preparation

The paper cups need to be filled with a little water (about one-quarter of a cup). There are a number of ways you can do this. The first way is to have the cups filled beforehand, placed on trays and ready to pass around just before the activity. Another way is to fill the cups beforehand, place them on a table near the entrance, and have students pick up a paper cup with water as they enter the room. Yet another method is to give each student a paper cup and then pass around pitchers of water.

how to play

Have the group assemble in the meeting room, and then give everyone a small paper cup with a little water in each. Tell the group that you are going to do a toast to commemorate something. Tell them that whoever does this toast exactly like you will win a special prize. Tell them to repeat everything you do.

Take your cup of water and hold it up in the air and say, "A toast." They'll repeat.

Continue: "To everyone here." (Move your cup to your left.) Let them repeat.

Then say, "And to everyone at home." (Move your cup to the right.) They repeat.

"And to the future." (Move your cup straight ahead again.) They repeat.

Then say "bottoms up!" and pour the water into your mouth, but rather than swallowing it, you'll actually keep the water in your mouth. Bring your hand with the cup in it down as if you've finished the toast and "swallowed" the water. Wait for the audience to do the same. When they are done, spit your water back into your cup (as if that were the real ending to the toast). Everyone will have already swallowed his or her water, and it will be too late to do anything about it. No prize winners!

number: **30+ people**

prep time: **none**

time required: **10-15 minutes**

8

duck, pig, cow

This works best for groups of 30 or more.

how to play

Assign one-third of your students to be ducks, another one-third to be pigs, and the remaining one-third to be cows. Tell them that the object of this game is to make their animal sounds as loud as they can and find the other animals. The trick is that they will do this in the dark. Turn out all the lights and tell them to walk around, making their sounds and locating the other group members making the same sound. When they find someone making the same sound, they form a group. That group stays together and continues to find more of the same. After several minutes, tell them you will turn on the lights and that they are to sit down with their group. The largest group wins. Be sure to do this in total darkness. A strobe light also works!

variations

- Use different animals and their sounds.
- Make up new and unusual sounds.
- Assign the participants things like foods or candy names or colors, and have them yell out their food/candy/color until they find their groups.

find and sign

number: **any size group**

prep time: **10-15 minutes**

time required: **15-20 minutes**

This activity can begin before your meeting starts as students are coming in and hanging out.

materials needed

Photocopies of "Find and Sign" sheet, enough for everyone in the group
Pens or pencils

preparation

Design a Find and Sign information sheet (see page 132) that applies to your group. Make enough photocopies so that every group member has one.

how to play

As students arrive, give each of them a Find and Sign information sheet. Instruct them to get as many signatures from other students as they can. The person with the most signatures wins. Remind the participants to only sign another's paper if they have honestly done the activity. When your meeting time starts, collect all of the papers and have an adult leader determine the winner.

Find and Sign

Your Name:_____

Find at least one person for each of the following categories and have each one sign beside the phrase that describes him or her.

Find Someone Who . . .

Has been to Europe _____

Is a junior in high school _____

Was born in Florida _____

Is wearing purple _____

Has a Beatles album _____

Likes spinach _____

Ate a hamburger last night _____

Won a beauty pageant _____

Can whistle _____

Hates chocolate _____

10

flour power

materials needed

10-pound bag of flour
A wooden board or sturdy cardboard
A large bowl
A small piece of wrapped candy
Table knife
A table

preparation

First, set up the table in front of the group. Take a large bowl and pack it up to the top very tightly with the flour. Place the board or sturdy cardboard on top of the bowl. While holding both together firmly, flip the bowl over and place the board on the table. Gently lift the bowl, leaving the flour on the table. If you packed it tightly enough, the flour should retain the shape of the bowl.

how to play

Gently place a small piece of candy on top of the flour. Next, line up everyone in single file. Give the first person in line a table knife and have him or her carve out a small part of the bowl-shaped pile of flour away from the candy. After each successful carving, have each person give the knife to the next person in line. This continues until the candy finally falls into the remaining flour, and then the person who made it fall must pick it out with his or her lips. The result is hilarious!

number: **any size group**

prep time: **10-15 minutes**

time required: **10-15 minutes**

cleanup: **slight**

number: **any size group**

prep time: **none**

time required: **10 minutes**

11

gorilla, gun, karate

This is a variation of the game "Rock, Paper, Scissors."

materials needed

Whiteboard or large sheets of paper
An appropriate writing instrument

preparation

Write the following words on the whiteboard or on the large sheets of paper:

> Gorilla kills gun
>
> Gun kills karate
>
> Karate kills gorilla

how to play

Have the group members find a partner and then stand back to back with their partner. When the leader yells "go," the students are to quickly turn around and act out one of the phrases. For the gorilla, they will make a gorilla stance and growl. For the gun, they point their finger and yell "bang." For karate, they are to strike a karate pose and yell "yaaah!" After they have done this, they look at the list to see who won. The losers sit and the winners find a new partner. This continues until there is one person left.

12

grab groups

number: **any size group**

prep time: **none**

time required: **10 minutes**

how to play

Explain to the group that they will walk around and mingle until you yell out a number. They are then to form a group with that number of people in it. For example, if you yell "six!" they must stop and grab five other people to form small groups of six members each. When they do form the group of six, they are to sit down. If any group has more or less than six people in the group, they are out of the game and must sit on the sidelines. Then when you say "mingle," they are to start mingling again until you call out another number. This is repeated until there are only two people left.

variation

You could expand on this idea by using this crowdbreaker as a means to form discussion groups. After calling out a number, ask the students to sit down together to discuss a statement, verse or question. The topics could range from silly to serious. This can be used to discuss one topic, or after a few minutes of discussion, you could ask them to get up and mingle again until you call another number and give them another topic.

number: **30+ people**

prep time: **none**

time required: **10-15 minutes**

cleanup: **slight**

13

head of lettuce

materials needed

A head of lettuce for every 12 to 15 students

how to play

Divide the group into smaller groups of approximately 12 to 15 students. Give each small group a fresh head of lettuce. Ask a student to carefully remove one entire leaf of lettuce and place it on the floor in front of him or her. Then have that student pass the head of lettuce on to the next person, who also removes a leaf. Continue around the circle until the head of lettuce is reduced to the heart. As the head goes around the circle, the leaves will become smaller. As each student removes a leaf, he or she should keep it in the order of removal.

After the head has been completely disassembled, announce that now the students need to reassemble the head of lettuce. Tell the students that when you shout "go," they will take the heart of the lettuce, place their leaf where it was, and pass it to the next person, until the head is reassembled.

Of course, this is impossible to accomplish, as there is no pinning or gluing of the leaves back to the heart. The point is to involve the students in an impossible yet hilarious activity.

tip

If any group decides to take this challenge seriously, the key to a level of success is in slowly reassembling the head, with each member being careful when he or she hands it off to the next person. This is a great way for the youth leaders to challenge the students to work together to solve a problem. Only the adults know the key—taking the time to do it right.

14

ice cream hunt

materials needed

Five gift certificates from a local ice cream or frozen yogurt shop

preparation

Before the crowdbreaker begins, have five students planted in the audience. Each of these students will have a gift certificate for the local ice cream or frozen yogurt shop (or a similar prize).

how to play

Ask students to stand, walk around and mingle. When the agreed-upon signal is given, have everyone stop where they are. Have the first person with a gift certificate shout out "Here I am!" and then give a gift certificate to the person next to him or her. Have the students mingle again and repeat. Do this five times.

number: **any size group**

prep time: **none**

time required: **10-15 minutes**

number: **any size group**

prep time: **5-10 minutes**

time required: **variable**

15

middle name tags

materials needed

Nametags

Felt-tip pens

how to play

Have the students write their middle names on their nametags, rather than their first and/or last names. If some of the students are too embarrassed to do this, ask them to place their middle initial on the tag. Occasionally, some students will have no middle name, so ask them to give themselves one that they would like.

Spend the rest of the meeting pointedly using as many middle names as possible. Require each student to refer to each other by his or her middle name. You can even have the students use their middle names when talking to you. You can set this up by repeatedly asking them, "What was your name again?"

16

my aunt came back

This is an audience participation song in which the joke is on the students! It's hard to teach a song without being there in person, but you can do it.

number: **any size group**

materials needed

A copy of the song (if you don't have it memorized)

prep time: **none**

how to play

In this song, the leader sings a line and then acts out a motion. The audience then mimics each line and motion. The results are hilarious. The leader announces that this is a song that requires audience participation. The tune could be anything you want, just keep it really simple so that the audience can repeat it easily.

time required: **10 minutes**

Leader sings:	"My aunt came back . . ."
Audience:	"My aunt came back . . ."
Leader:	"From Kalamazoo."
Audience:	"From Kalamazoo."
Leader:	"She brought with her . . ."
Audience:	"She brought with her . . ."
Leader:	"Some gum to chew." *At this point begin making an exaggerated chewing motion as if you were chewing a huge piece of gum. The audience should do the same.*
Audience:	"Some gum to chew."

That was the first line of five lines. Sing each line and act out the motion with the audience repeating after you.

Line two:	"My aunt came back . . ."
	Audience repeats.
	"From New Orleans."
	Audience repeats.

139

"She brought with her . . ."
Audience repeats.
"A pair of jeans." *Hit your hip with your hand and entice the audience to do the same. You and the audience should be chewing gum and hitting your hip all at the same time. Audience repeats.*

Line three:

"My aunt came back . . ."
Audience repeats.
"From Niagara Falls."
Audience repeats.
"She brought with her . . ."
Audience repeats.
"Some ping-pong balls." *Sway left to right as if you where watching a ping-pong game being played (or as if you were playing ping-pong). Now, you and the audience should be chewing, hitting your hips, and swaying your head from side to side. Audience repeats.*

Line four:

"My aunt came back . . ."
Audience repeats.
"From the New York Fair."
Audience repeats.
"She brought with her . . ."
Audience repeats.
"A rocking chair." *Now rock back and forth while at the same time chewing, hitting your hips, and swaying your head from side to side. Audience repeats.*

Line five:

"My aunt came back . . ."
Audience repeats.
"From Timbuktu." *Audience repeats.*
"She brought with her . . ."
Audience repeats.
"Some NUTS LIKE YOU!" *Point at the audience as you say this!*

Stop everything and point to the audience! The joke's on them!

17

nametag puzzle match

number: **any size group**

materials needed

Nametags
Felt-tip pens
Scissors

prep time: **15-30 minutes**

preparation

Prior to the meeting, cut each nametag into two pieces, making different jagged, curved or zigzag cuts on each one. On the two pieces, write names that can be split into two parts but that share similar endings. For example, there are several superheroes whose names end in "man," "woman," "boy" or "girl," such as Superman, Wonder Woman, Spiderman, Batman and Bat Girl.

time required: **15 minutes**

how to play

As the students gather, have them select a piece of nametag puzzle. When they find the person who matches the other half, that person becomes their partner for the evening.

variation

You could also use famous people who share the same last names. You can get names from collections of biographies. It's okay if the students don't know the name, because they can find the match by fitting the two puzzle pieces together.

number: **any size group**

prep time: **none**

time required: **5-10 minutes**

18

one match

materials needed

A large box of wooden matches

how to play

Have the students sit in a circle and then give a match to each student. One at a time, have each student light his or her match and name off as many facts about himself or herself before the match burns out (or he or she blows it out). If you have a group of 20 or more, have the students form smaller groups of 8 to 10 to do this activity.

19

onion toss

materials needed

A peeled onion
A stereo, CD player or musical instrument
Music to play

how to play

Have the group sit down in a circle. Another person needs to control the music source—a stereo, CD player or a musical instrument. In all fairness, the person playing the music should not be able to see who has the onion. Tell the group that while the music is playing, an onion is going to be passed around the circle. When the music stops, the person who is left holding the onion must take a bite. After the bite has been taken, the music begins and the onion is tossed again, and the process starts all over. Do this six to eight times.

number: **any size group**

prep time: **1-5 minutes**

time required: **10 minutes**

20

partners

how to play

Have each student choose a partner. Have each pair stand back to back. On the count of three, instruct them to turn around and do one of the following contests (leader's choice):

- Each partner indicates a number with his or her fingers, and then they add the numbers. The first one to add correctly wins and finds a new partner. The losers sit down on the sidelines.

- Each partner indicates a number with his or her fingers, and then they multiply the numbers. The first one finished wins. The losers sit down on the sidelines.

- Each partner indicates a number with his or her fingers, and then they subtract the difference between the numbers. The first one finished wins. The losers sit down on the sidelines.

- Each partner faces each other and plays a thumb war. The losers sit down on the sidelines.

Eliminate the losers each time, and have students form pairs with new partners until there is only one student left.

21

roll sharing

number: **any size group**

materials needed

A roll or two of toilet paper (depending on the size of the group)

prep time: **none**

how to play

Have students form a circle, either standing or sitting. Pass around a roll of toilet paper, telling the students, "Take any number of pieces of toilet paper, up to 10 pieces." Give no further instructions. After everyone has his or her sheet of toilet paper, announce that for every sheet of toilet paper each group member has selected, he or she must share something about himself or herself that the other group members don't know. As each person shares, he or she rips off one piece of toilet paper and throws it into the center.

time required: **15-20 minutes**

tip

This activity works best if each student shares only one piece of information at a time, giving students a chance to build on the other students' ideas and stories.

number: **any size group**

prep time: **none**

time required: **10 minutes**

22

scar show and tell

how to play

Have group members show and tell their war stories about the scars that they *can* show to everyone in the room. Sharing the stories of wounds can be a very meaningful and even emotional time. It can also be simply goofy, because many scars may simply be due to the person's silly mistakes. Whatever the reason, these little, brief times of sharing help students to know more about one another and promote a sense of unity and a we-are-in-this-life-together attitude.

23

snowball fight

materials needed

Volleyball net or long rope
Bedsheets, tarps or painters' dropcloths
A large amount of newspapers (collected ahead of time)

preparation

Begin to collect the newspapers a few weeks before you do this activity. Divide the playing area by stringing a volleyball net or long rope across the center. The divider should only be about three or four feet high. Drape bedsheets or other large pieces of cloth over the net (or rope) so that the two teams cannot see each other when they are seated on the floor or ground.

how to play

Divide your group into two equal teams. Have each team sit on opposite sides of the draped net or rope. Give each group a large stack of newspapers and tell them they are going to have a snowball fight. Tell them that on your signal they are to wad up newspaper "snowballs" and throw the snowballs at the other team. After a few minutes, stop the action and decide which team has the least amount of paper snowballs on its side of the net. That team is declared the winner (or, if you're doing this several times, give that team a point). Continue this as long as time allows or when one team reaches a certain score.

number: **any size group**

prep time: **10-15 minutes**

time required: **10-20 minutes**

cleanup: **slight**

number: **any size group**

prep time: **none**

time required: **10-15 minutes**

24

sprees!

materials needed

A large bag of M&Ms, Skittles or other multi-colored candy

how to play

Give everyone an M&M, Skittle or other multi-colored candy as they walk in the door. Tell them to memorize their color and then eat the candy. After everyone has arrived, explain the game. Tell them that when all of the lights go out, they are to yell out their color and find as many other people with their color as they can and form a group by interlocking arms. Turn off the lights quickly before they have time to begin looking for friends and asking them their color. After a few minutes, turn the lights back on and see which group is the largest. The chaos is wild and crazy fun.

25

toss up

number: **any size group**

prep time: **none**

time required: **10 minutes**

how to play

Have the group form smaller groups of 5 to 10 members. All groups must have the same number of students. Next, have one person in each group lie down. The rest of the group will pick up that person, throw him or her into the air *and* catch the person. Then have the groups do the same thing to every other person in their small group. They will continue to do this until everyone in the group has been thrown into the air and caught. The first group to finish throwing each person wins.

tip

Advise students to do this activity in a reasonable manner so that no one is hurt.

number: **any size group**

prep time: **none**

time required: **10 minutes**

26

touch

preparation

Remove any obstacles or anything that is breakable from the play area.

how to play

Have everyone line up in one straight line down the middle of your room. Have the other adult leaders stand around to judge which student is last and whether or not each student gets back into line correctly. Instruct the group that you will call out an object or place and that when you say "go," they are to run and touch that object or place. The following are some examples of objects or places to use:

- Touch the front door.
- Touch Jim's hat.
- Touch Pastor Bob.
- Touch Mary's foot.
- Touch the back door and the ping-pong table.

The last student to make it back into his or her spot is out. Continue this until there is only one student left.

27

towel toss

This is a fast, action-packed game and can last for any length of time you choose.

materials needed

A towel

how to play

Have the whole group form one huge circle and sit down. Select one student to sit in the middle—this student will be It. Give the towel to one of the students sitting in the circle. When you say go, It is to try to get the towel or touch one of the people who is holding the towel while everyone else in the circle tries his or her best to get rid of the towel by throwing it around the circle. If the person in the middle catches the towel, the person who threw it then becomes It.

variations

You can add variations such as using two towels, or a ball and a towel, or a ball and a shirt. Use your imagination!

number: **any size group**

prep time: **none**

time required: **10-15 minutes**

number: **any size group**

prep time: **none**

time required: **10-15 minutes**

28

trains

This works best with large groups—in fact, the larger the better.

how to play

Have the group form a large circle. Choose three to four leaders who will be the first "Engines." The Engines will chugga-chugga-chug to another person in the circle, grab him or her by the shoulders, and ask his or her name. When the person says his or her name, the Engine will hop on one leg and say the person's name. Then, the Engine hops on the other leg and says the person's name. He or she does this for a total of five hops on each leg.

After the fifth time, the two people form a two-person train, with the new person becoming the Engine at the front and the other person holding on to the shoulders of the new Engine. The trains will each move to another student in the circle. The process then repeats: the Engine asks the person's name, he or she says the name while hopping five times, and then the new person becomes the Engine of the train. After a few minutes, huge trains of students are formed that run around and through each other.

29

trivia warm-up

number: **any size group**

prep time: **10-15 minutes**

time required: **15-20 minutes**

This activity makes a good transition between a rowdy time and a quieter time such as between game time and Bible study.

materials needed

A few selected trivia questions
Small pieces of candy
Three large candy bars

preparation

Go online, browse your local library or use some of those old Trivial Pursuit® game cards and come up with at least nine random trivia questions to ask your students. You will use two as practice questions and one as a winner question. The practice questions should be a little easier (and hopefully a little bizarre). After the two practice cards, select a winner question, which should be more difficult and hopefully even a little more bizarre.

how to play

Tell students that they are going to play a trivia icebreaker. You will read two practice questions, and whoever shouts out the correct answer gets a piece of candy (or other small treat) thrown to them. After completing the first two practice questions, inform the students that you will now read the winning question and that whoever shouts out the correct answer gets a full-size candy bar (or team points). Continue to alternate: two practice questions, one winner question; two practice, one winner question; and so on.

tip

This is also a good activity to do around a heavy academic time of the school year for the students, such as during finals or when school is about to start.

number: **any size group**

prep time: **10-15 minutes**

time required: **10-15 minutes**

30

what matches?

materials needed

Chalkboard, whiteboard or sheet of newsprint

preparation

Write the following statements on the board or on the sheet of newsprint:

- Who I am, really.
- Who others seem to think I am.
- My most important goal.

how to play

As the students gather, tell them that they will be paired up in various ways and will share their answers to the three questions with several different groups of people. To get them to mix, prepare a number of criteria. For example, have them find one other person . . .

- With the same color of pants/skirt or shirt/top
- With or without words printed on their T-shirts
- Wearing the same amount or kinds of jewelry
- With or without braces
- With or without glasses
- With the same hair color
- In the same grade level in school
- With the same favorite soda flavor
- With the same favorite sport
- With or without toenail polish color

Call out a category and watch to see that the students pair up with one other person who meets the criteria. If you have uneven numbers, allow three people to team up. Then have them share their responses to the three questions with each other. When everyone has shared, call out a new category and have the students find a new partner.

31

what's important?

number: **any size group**

This crowdbreaker will always get total participation from the students. It has never failed to create the feelings it is designed to create.

prep time: **none**

materials needed

A large quantity of 3x5-inch index cards or slips of paper, 10 per person
Pens or pencils

time required: **15-20 minutes**

how to play

Have everyone sit in a large circle, preferably on the floor. Give everyone in the room 10 3x5-inch index cards (or slips of paper) and a pen or pencil. Have the students write the 10 most important things in their life, one item per card (for example, their family, God, their dog, their Bible, their health, and so forth). You can prime their thoughts with a few suggestions.

When they are done writing on the cards, have them turn their cards face down and shuffle them so that they have no idea what cards are where in the stack. **Very important:** Do not let them look at what is written on the cards once they are shuffled.

Now say something like, "Martians have just come into our town. They come to your homes and hold each of you at laser gunpoint, demanding that you give up the top three cards on your stack. Without looking at them, pull off the top three cards. You no longer have these things. The Martians have taken them from you."

There will be many moans and groans from the youth, and they will not want to give up some of the things that the Martians have taken from them. Have them read their cards to themselves as they throw the cards one at a time into the center of the circle. Ask them to take a look at the seven items they still have.

Next, say something like, "Just when you are getting over the shock of the loss of those three things, a roving band of Plutonians comes to your door. They demand money from you, but you have none. They say, 'Give us two items of your choice, and we won't torch your house!' Now, pick out two of your remaining cards and throw them into the middle of the room. After you give the Plutonians your two items, they leave you alone." Now have the students shuffle the cards face down once again.

Keep going along these same lines, alternating back and forth between discarding cards according to choice and then without looking at the cards. Make up another story each time (natural disasters, burglars, or other crisis). Stop when students each have only two cards left, and then make them choose between the two.

tip

There are a number of different directions this activity can lead. It can be used as a springboard for a discussion on priorities, on the illusion of the control we have over our own lives, on how cushy our lives are compared to people in the rest of the world. This activity can result in the students exploring what it feels like to experience disastrous loss. There are groans of anguish as the students struggle with losing the things listed on their cards. It also helps them take a look at what has lasting value over things that are less important.

32

where I've been

number: **20+ people**

prep time: **10-15 minutes**

time required: **15-30 minutes**

materials needed

Several maps of the United States/the world, one map for about 10 students
Straight pins or push pins
Small slips of paper
Paper
Pens or pencils

preparation

Attach the maps to walls around the room.

how to play

Give each student 10 straight pins or push pins, a pen or pencil, and 10 slips of paper. Tell students to write their names on their 10 slips of paper, and then stick a pin through the end of each tag.

Have students pair up and talk about their travels with their partners. They can describe their favorite vacation spot, the most exotic location they have visited, the farthest or longest trip they have taken, or anything else related to their travel experiences. After they share with their partners, have them list their top 10 favorite places. Have the pairs team up with four other pairs to form groups of 10, and then have each group of 10 gather around one of the maps taped to the walls around the room. After everyone has made their lists, have each person push the pins with their names attached into the maps to show how much and how far group members have traveled.

To close, form a prayer circle and lead the students in praying for those people they met on their trips and to challenge them to see their future travels as opportunities for sharing the Good News throughout the world.

tip

This activity can lead into the topic of world evangelism, or similar topics relevant to the call of the Church to go into the world and share their faith.

number: **any size group**

prep time: **15-30 minutes**

time required: **5-10 minutes**

33

who am I?

This is a great crowdbreaker to get students to mingle.

materials needed

Sticky notes or small slips of paper

preparation

On the sticky notes or slips of paper, write the names of several characters from cartoons, TV shows, movies, books, the Bible or any other similar source that will provide characters the group will be able to identify. Write down enough characters so that each group member has one.

how to play

As group members arrive, stick the notes (or pin the slips of paper) on each person's back so that he or she cannot see the name. The object of the game is for each person to figure out who he or she is by asking other members yes or no questions about his or her character. For example, if the category is TV shows, the members will want to begin by asking general questions: "Am I in a cartoon?" "Am I on a sitcom?" "Am I a male or female character?" When the participants guess their names correctly, have them give you the piece of paper. They will then continue to help others find out who they really are. Limit the time to about 10 minutes or less.

34

word of the week

number: **any size group**

prep time: **10-15 minutes**

time required: **10 minutes**

This fun icebreaker is a real groaner.

materials needed

Chalk or whiteboard, posterboard, or large sheet of paper
Appropriate writing instrument
Wild clothing and props for a crazy costume

preparation

Select someone—a student or an adult—to become your Word Wizard, Word Nerd, or some other silly name. Dress this person as a wacky character (such as a nutty professor with a commencement robe and mortarboard, a nerdy person or a crazy magician). Give this person the word list so that he or she can prepare each week.

how to play

Tell the whole group that you have brought in an expert to help them with their SAT scores and that you are beginning a new program called the "Word of the Week." Introduce your guest, and then have that person come forward and introduce that week's word. Have him or her do each of the following:

1. Write the Word of the Week on the chalkboard, whiteboard or piece of paper up front.

2. Define the word.

3. Use the word in a sentence. For example: "Today's word is 'gorilla.' Gorilla means 'to cook by gentle heating.'" A sample sentence: "Honey, will you please make me a gorilla cheese sandwich?"

Now listen to the group groan.

tip

Be sure to use *the* Word of the Week in the sample sentence. For example, do not say "grilled" instead of "gorilla," because that would ruin the absurdity of the joke. Also, make sure that you continue the Word of the Week activity for several weeks.

other words of the week

- Declare—"cloudlessness" (the clear)
- Diploma—"one who fixes the sink" (the plumber)
- Enunciate—"what gave the cannibal an upset stomach" (a nun she ate)
- Europe—"out of bed early" (you're up)
- European—"an insult" (you're a pain)
- Excel—"the price of eggs" (eggs sell)
- Granite—"to disregard or forget about" (granted)
- Gruesome—"to grow in size or number" (grew some)
- Handsome—"to pass along" (hand some)
- Harmonious—"location of our funds" (our money is)
- Intense—"where we sleep on a camping trip" (in tents)
- Isolate—"excuse for not being on time" (I so late)
- Khaki—"small metal object that starts a car" (car key)
- Officiate—"seafood eaten" (a fish he ate)
- Token—"speaking" (talking)

Community Builders

community \ke myü ne te\ *n* **1 a** : a unified body of individuals **b**: a group of people with a common characteristic or interest living together within a larger society.

builder \bil der\ *n* **1** : one that builds, especially: one that contracts to build and supervises builder operations.

number: **any size group**

prep time: **60+ minutes**

time required: **30-60 minutes**

1

alternative popularity contest

Traditionally, the measures of teenage popularity have been attached to scholastic or athletic ability, good looks, best clothing sense and other superficial criteria. Admittedly, these standards leave many, if not most, teenagers on the outside looking in at the popular circles. The usual criteria for popularity represent only a fraction of the total abilities that can be found in any group of people. So to break the molds and spotlight all of the students in your group, try an Alternative Popularity Contest.

materials needed

Photocopies of ballots
Pens or pencils
Nomination sheets
Transparent tape or masking tape
Several tables
Ballot containers for each category (small boxes or baskets)

preparation

This activity is longer than most and takes some planning. It will occupy a whole meeting and will require about an hour for a group of 30 people to complete. It also needs to include a game or snack break. However, it is well worth the time and preparation.

Advertise that in this meeting, everyone will have a chance to be recognized by his or her peers for the great gifts God that has given each person. Brainstorm with other adult leaders, or through contacting parents, categories of giftedness that are found among the youth group members. (See the list of possible suggestions following these directions.)

Prepare ballots with categories ahead of time and photocopy enough for everyone. Then prepare blank ballots for write-in nominations and a sign-in sheet for all the students to sign as they enter the meeting (so that adult leaders can make sure each student receives an award).

what to do

You will need lots of ballots and pens or pencils for this community builder. Post each category on the nomination sheets hung on the walls or placed on tables around the room. List the category in large print at the top of the sheet. Each voter will write his or her nomination for each category on these nomination sheets. The nomination sheets look best when produced with a computer, but handwritten nomination categories will work just fine. You will need to provide extra blank sheets for added category ideas.

Nominating occurs when each student reads a category and then nominates one person for each category. Each participant should walk from sheet to sheet, deciding who to choose for each category, and then write down one nomination for each category. Place ballots in a container located under each category sheet.

Have other adult leaders tally the votes and award the title to the candidate with the most votes. Each student should only win one award. When someone wins a category, record his or her name on a list to be announced later. The goal will be to make sure that every student gets an award, so the leaders will need to be aware of what is going on and have some categories ready to add or give credit to the ones who may be overlooked. If you plan the program well, every student will get nominated for something.

Have a standard certificate ready and fill it in, noting the winner's name and the category. Put some affirming language in a certificate similar to the one on page 166.

how to begin

When the group is assembled, tell them, "Each of us is a special creation of God. In His limitless variety, God has given us a unique blend of gifts and attributes. Unfortunately, our society focuses on only a very few of the more superficial measures of popularity: the size and shape of our bodies, our looks, the sports we play, our clothes, our grades, and the like. However, tonight we will be recognizing and awarding other types of achievement. On with the show!"

Next, instruct the students how to do the voting. Distribute pens or pencils and let the students walk around and browse the categories. They may nominate themselves or a friend for any listed category. With advisor approval, they may add a new category for nominations.

After nominations are closed, the students will vote (one vote per nomination category). Adult leaders will then need to count the votes in a location where they cannot be seen by the students, and make a list with a winner for each category. Provide a snack, game time or other activity while the counting is being done. Leaders should list only one person per category—don't allow multiple winners. Also, leaders should check the winners with the sign-in sheet to make sure that each student receives an award. If a student wins in more than one category, have the leaders choose the most appropriate one to award that student. Then award the other categories to the second- or third-place nominees. In other words, if Jane has won three different awards, give her the category most befitting her, and award the other two categories to someone else who was nominated but did not have the most votes. It is much easier than it sounds!

Complete the event with an awards ceremony and lots of affirmations and applause. Close with a prayer thanking God for investing so much in each person and for allowing everyone to grow together as a group.

suggested categories

Best joke teller	Greatest knowledge of Scripture
Most interesting dresser	Most colorful clothing
Best bargain shopper	Cleanest car
Knows the most trivia	Most artistic
Most active in worship	Owns the most hats
Biggest sports fan	Most adventuresome
Greatest animal lover	Newest to the youth group
Best musician	Strongest witness for Christ
Most volunteerism at church	Best storyteller
Best evangelist	Hardest worker
Most community service	Best cook
Best natural comic ability	Quickest with a quip or comeback
Best laugh	Always smells good
Most fitting name	Best hairdo
Kindest	Friendliest
Fastest talker	Safest driver
Most athletic	Most courageous
Asks the best questions	Greatest technology expert
Best singer	Most positive
Most Christlike servant	Most helpful

Most joyful

Most compassionate

Best businessperson

Most honest

Most generous

Most inventive

Try to focus on positive attributes, and tailor-make plenty of categories to fit your group.

you are special!

_____,

recognizing that you are blessed with many good attributes

and specially gifted by God, you have been chosen by your fellow

youth group members and leaders to be especially honored

for your special gift of

_____

On this day _____

Signed _____

2

an "it's not my birthday!" birthday

number: **any size group**

prep time: **none**

time required: **30-60 minutes**

When you and your students are on the road for mission trips or work camps, it's fun to treat them to at least one nice meal—usually in a fun place such as a Hard Rock Cafe or a Planet Hollywood-type restaurant. After the meal, honor one of the older students—usually one who is graduating and will soon be heading away to college—with a birthday cake and have the servers sing "Happy Birthday" to him or her. Of course, make sure that the honoree's actual birthday is a few months away, and never give clues as to who the target will be.

This is one of those affirming fun things that will remain in the memories of the whole group for a long time. It will become a strong group builder, because it is just one of those wild things that the students can look forward to. It also lends itself to the community spirit of fun on trips. The honorees always feel a degree of honor (after they recover from the slight embarrassment), so you may want to pick one of the more peripheral students who may not have shone as brightly as some of the youth group stars. It can become a badge of great recognition to be picked.

number: **8+ people**

prep time: **30+ minutes**

time required: **60 minutes**

3

curriculum creations

This community builder will require a few weeks to come to completion. Don't be afraid to dedicate a month's worth of meetings to the program. It will develop relationships and leadership among small groups, who in turn will share their creation with the larger group.

materials needed

Old Sunday School/youth ministry curriculum
Scissors
Transparent tape/glue
Pens and pencils
Paper
Felt-tip pens
Newsprint

preparation

Prior to the first week, gather as much old Sunday School and youth ministry curriculum as you can. Anything from decades ago up to the previous year will do. Then gather all of the supplies on tables in the middle of the youth group meeting area.

what to do

Divide the students into small groups consisting of four to seven members. Tell them that they have the assignment of developing a youth group meeting that they will lead in the weeks to come. Help them to understand the various elements of the meetings that they will lead. Let them mix up the order or change some elements if they want.

You may want to suggest something like the following outline:

- Opening activity (a game or icebreaker)
- Worship/Music
- Introduction activity for study

- The Bible lesson/study
- Discussion
- Wrap-up
- Snack
- Closing prayer

Add or delete any other elements that you use or don't use.

Instruct the students to go through the curricula on the tables to get ideas on how to conduct the kind of meeting they wish to lead—with the catch that in the coming weeks, they will actually lead the meeting they have created.

tip

Most of the students, if not all, will take this assignment very seriously. Do not interpret attempts at being creative with cutting up. Some groups, if they get in a jam, may try to act as if they don't care or will goof off to cover their frustrations or embarrassment. Be ready to help interpret, support, bail out or modify. Let them know you are available to advise when they have a problem, but avoid working out their difficulties for them.

This activity has promise on so many levels. Don't be afraid to try it! Some of the benefits may be that the students will have a better appreciation for the difficulty of your job, you may gain some insight into what interests them, and you will discover potential new group leaders.

number: **any size group**

prep time: **5-10 minutes**

time required: **none during meeting**

4

email prayer list

Teenagers around the country are logging zillions of hours emailing and texting each other. While this packs its own concerns, it may also hold some uncharted possibilities.

materials needed

Computers or cell phones with online service

what to do

Establish an online prayer-concerns list to be emailed to the addresses of your youth group members. When you hear of a need, post it for all of the students who are online. The hope is that they will read it, pray for the needy person, and then log a response to him or her or to other group members. Eventually, the students will begin posting their own entries and concerns.

It is important to check the email every day or so to make sure that you as the initiator are aware of what the students are posting. This is not because of them posting bad stuff, but because they will need to know that you, too, are using the email and praying for them.

This is also a somewhat anonymous way for quiet students who never ask for prayer to make their needs for prayer known to others. You may need to educate some students on the use of the email address book or on other ways that they can send a note or message to everyone in the group.

5

freshmen no more

number: **any size group**

prep time: **10 minutes**

time required: **60+ minutes**

It is hard to get away from identifying students in a high school group by something other than their grade level. Yet for younger students especially, acceptance as an equal is a very important factor in them feeling that they are part of the group. At school, freshmen are often the focus of unkind jokes, pranks or comments. Many feel insecurity, or even terror, at leaving middle or junior high school for the perils of high school.

Your youth group needs to be a welcoming and comforting place for freshmen. However, if your group members refer to them as "freshmen," it will leave them with the impression that they are not part of the group—or at least that they are on probation for a year before being fully accepted.

In your first meeting or activity when the freshmen join the youth group for the first time, divide all of the students into the four corners of the room by grade. Beginning with the seniors, introduce each person and applaud the whole bunch. Then introduce the juniors, the sophomores, and finally the freshmen.

Next, ask the other three grades to mingle with the freshmen, learn their names, introduce themselves and personally welcome each new student. After this mingling has happened, have each older student pick a freshman as his or her guest for the evening and eat a meal together.

Follow this up with games, maybe a brief Bible devotion, and other features such as reviewing the coming year's schedule and making announcements. At the end of the evening, have all of the freshmen stand inside a circle of the older students, and then say a prayer of thanksgiving to God for blessing your group with such a wonderfully gifted set of new members. Then give the following announcement:

Tonight you came to us as freshmen. You are new to our group, and there are still some things we need to share with you and that you need to share with us. In the months to come, we are going to get to know you better. We'll learn your names and what you like to do. We'll go on trips together and study God's Word with you. But that is hard to do if we all look at you as underclassmen. In Christ, there is no east or west, no male and female and no class divisions. We are all His children. Therefore, from this night on, you will no longer be called "freshmen." The name is gone. From now on, you are our sisters and brothers in Christ and an important part of this group. The designation of freshman is gone. Welcome to youth group.

This is even more impressive if a senior or junior says it. How many of those freshmen do you think will be back next week? How many of them will want to bring a friend?

6

GiG

number: **any size group**

prep time: **5-15 minutes**

time required: **60+ minutes**

For the most part, any high school group functions well as a large group. But there are problems, at times, with different ages understanding the challenges of a student just entering high school and one about to graduate. Some of the older students may quit participating in youth group if they cannot relate to the younger students who seem so immature to them.

In one group, the youth pastor called a meeting of the eleventh and twelfth graders to decide what they could do about this problem. The youth pastor told the group members that their leadership and experience were needed as an example of maturity for the younger students. He proposed having a second meeting that would meet twice a month, which eventually became "Group-in-Group," or GiG. This concept works, and has in some ways revolutionized the youth ministry. As a community-building experience, it has strengthened the relationships of the older students with the younger, as well as the youth leader's relationship with all the students.

At GiG, the group discusses issues that are more relevant to the lives of those looking at graduation and college. They meet to discuss a proposed topic or agenda, and then the youth leader lets the students' discussions meander as they please, just as long as they remain relevant or important to their faith and walk with Christ. The group meets in homes, which seems to encourage more openness.

This model is highly recommended for any moderate- to large-sized youth program.

number: **any size group**

prep time: **20 minutes**

time required: **60-90 minutes**

7

gratitude pictures

This activity takes about an hour to an hour and a half to complete.

materials needed

Several 9x12-inch sheets of colored construction paper, one sheet
 per student
Several pairs of scissors
Several bottles of glue, or glue sticks
A large stack of old magazines
A small slip of paper for each student
A box, or similar container, to hold slips of paper

what to do

As the students gather, have each of them write their names on slips of paper and put them into a box, hat or other similar container. When the meeting begins, have each person choose a name from the container. Instruct the students that they are to keep the name they chose to themselves.

Tell students they will cut or tear pictures from the magazines that describe the person whose name they picked. If anyone is stymied by the name picked because he or she doesn't know the person at all, he or she may trade for another name with the help of the leaders. In that situation, it is best to gather several of the names and have several students redraw names.

The students should note the great, wonderful, unique, gifted things about the person as they choose pictures or words from the magazines. The aim is to thank God through illustrative affirmations about the person being depicted. The activity becomes a guessing game when the whole group is invited to figure out who is being portrayed. Each "artist" may point out what is being depicted about the person.

tip

If visitors are in attendance, the person bringing the visitor may need to trade names with the guest so that he or she is not left out.

8

human bingo

number: **any size group**

Some might consider Human Bingo to be an icebreaker, but any time teenagers are discovering this much information about each other, you're building community.

prep time: **15 minutes**

materials needed

Photocopies of your customized Bingo sheets
Pens or pencils

preparation

time required: **10-15 minutes**

Customize the Bingo sheet to make it appropriate for your group (see page 176 for a sample sheet). At the top of each of the 4x4 squares, write various common or wacky questions to ask the participants. As you put the sheet together, think about what is relevant to the current or recent experiences of the teenagers in your group.

what to do

Tell the students that they are to collect signatures of other group members who fit into each of the Bingo categories. Set a time limit for them to gather signatures—less than 10 minutes works best. When the time is up, collect the sheets and have another youth worker decide the winner. The first to complete the whole sheet or to have the most rows or columns completed is the winner. (Instead of a time limit, you could have the first one to complete two rows or columns or the whole sheet shout "Bingo!")

variation

Assign a category to each of the four columns, such as "My Favorite Sport," "My Worst Color," or "My Dream Vacation." Then have each student write his or her own response in the first square under each category. Give them a time limit (five to seven minutes) to find other members with the same or similar answers to sign the three squares below each of their answers.

175

Human Bingo

Collect one signature for each square. Signatures must include both the first and last names.

Leisure Activities	Personal	Likes and Dislikes	Miscellaneous
Hasn't watched TV in more than 2 days	Has both a brother and a sister	Is radically committed to Jesus	Is wearing something with a logo
Has been snow skiing or snowboarding during the past year	Does not snore!	Loves to sing	Has his or her own car
Plays basketball on a school team	Is new to the group in the last month	Likes to eat broccoli	
Plays a musical instrument	Sings in the shower	Dislikes hip-hop music	

Human Bingo

Collect one signature for each square. Signatures must include both the first and last names.

Leisure Activities	Personal	Likes and Dislikes	Miscellaneous

number: **any size group**

prep time: **30-90 minutes**

time required: **60+ minutes**

9

indoor campout

This event is a blast when the winter months set in and your students get cabin fever. It works as an all-day activity, an overnighter or a long meeting. The more time spent on the activity, the better the effect. So when the students get stir crazy, nothing helps more than an Indoor Campout that involves them in games, singing, sharing, eating and all the rest of the things we love about camping.

materials needed

A few tents
Artificial/real trees and plants
Sleeping bags
Rocks, fireplace logs, red spotlight or red cellophane (for fake campfire)

what to do

The first step in having a successful Indoor Campout is to create the right atmosphere. Generally, people go camping in the forest in tents. Therefore, your goal will be to create a forest and provide tents for your students. Surprisingly, a forest is not hard to create. Many people today have artificial Christmas trees stored in the attic. Borrow as many as you can from church families or ask large department stores to let you use their display Christmas trees. Set up the trees in your youth room or fellowship hall. Put the trees in groupings of three or so with varying heights. You can also collect artificial or real potted plants to add to the outdoor feeling.

Borrow some tents as well. Note that you will not need to have enough tents for all of the students, because they will not be sleeping in them. However, you do need enough to create the feel of a campsite.

Other props and accessories that can be used to create atmosphere include fake snow, stuffed animals, the sound of running water and singing birds, and a campfire. Of course, it's not recommended that you start a real fire in your church! A realistic campfire can be made from a circle of stones, some real pieces of wood and a red spotlight or red cellophane paper.

Generally, a camping theme can be integrated into your usual favorite games and activities. Pin the Tail on the Bear and the Tent and Sleeping Bag Relays in the Games section of this book are especially good to play during this event. Use your creativity to adapt other games to the camping theme.

Food can also follow the camping theme. Make stew or spaghetti. Hot dogs or hamburgers are also appropriate. S'mores and mountain pies (pie filling cooked between pieces of bread) are common camping desserts that can be made in a conventional or microwave oven or indoor grill.

You can't go camping without singing camp songs around the fire. Pick your favorites, find a guitar player and enjoy yourself! You could have a time of testimony around the "fire." Present a youth talk about commitment and open up a time for sharing.

tip

The success of this activity is not so much the specifics of the camping atmosphere as it is a vehicle by which your group can become closer. Using the novel theme of indoor camping, nearly any topic can be adapted into a fun experience, and it is guaranteed to keep the attention of your students.

number: **any size group**

prep time: **15 minutes**

time required: **30 minutes**

cleanup: **slight**

10

let us bake bread together

If your group does daylong planning sessions, you can mix the planning time with a great mission project.

materials needed

Several bread-making machines
Ingredients needed for making bread (check machine recipes)

preparation

Borrow as many bread-making machines as you can and provide enough ingredients to make a loaf of bread in each of the machines.

what to do

Before the planning or leadership activity, assemble the group and have the students combine the ingredients and put them into the bread-making machines. While the bread is baking, have your planning meeting. Most machines take three to four hours to bake a loaf, so you will have plenty of time to plan.

When the bread is baked, harvest your labors, clean the kitchen and deliver the bread to someone in your church, such as new members, the ill or the elderly. This is a good way to build rapport, underscore the concept of missions, and give the students an opportunity to start and finish a project together—all of which build community unity.

tip

This community builder also provides an excellent opportunity to discuss the significance of bread in Communion or various references to the symbolism of bread in the New Testament.

11

lost civilization

number: **20+ people**

prep time: **5 minutes**

time required: **60 minutes**

One idea for a great small-group builder is to have the group develop conclusions together about what future archaeologists and sociologists will think about their culture.

materials needed

Paper

Pens or pencils

what to do

Divide students into 4 or 5 small groups (more are fine if your group is large). Ideally, there should be 5 to 10 students per group. Say the following to the groups:

> Tonight, you will create a reality that will be interpreted by a group of searching archaeologists from the year A.D. 2200 as they discover this area. Each group's members are permitted to wander around the church, and each person is to bring back an item that represents our group/culture. You may bring anything you can carry that is not obviously going to get us in trouble. You may also gather things from outside the building. Assemble your things in an interesting display in the center of the meeting room, and then create a story that describes how you use these gathered symbols or items. Write down the story and return to this room.

Assign a room or an area of a room to each small group for gathering their items and writing their story. Give the groups a time limit to complete their display and their story—about 30 to 45 minutes should be plenty of time. When the groups have collected and arranged their objects and written their stories, have them return to your meeting area.

The adult leaders should then lead the groups on a tour of the ancient remains of a recently discovered lost civilization. Supply each of your advisor archaeologists with a cap or distinctive hat, a magnifying glass and other campy uniform decorations. Lead the whole group from room to room and interpret the collected artifacts. Use humor, past history courses, folklore or whatever else you can think up to explain each collection. Then, after you have summed it all up, read newly discovered manuscripts—their written explanations—and see how close your conclusions about their displays were.

tip

This activity is great for building camaraderie as the groups put their stories together and listen as the whole group discusses their findings.

12

love songs

number: **any size group**

prep time: **30-60 minutes**

time required: **60 minutes**

For this activity, you will need access to a fairly large activity room.

materials needed

Several writable CDs
Several CD players
Paper
Pens or pencils
Transparent tape

preparation

Before the meeting, record parts of several songs on separate CDs (you can also use a tape player and record the songs on separate cassette tapes). Select from contemporary pop songs, standards, oldies or other music that the students will recognize. The songs should say something about love. In addition, select one good Christian song that has a love theme. Put the CDs and CD players in different locations around the meeting place or around the church.

Prepare a copy of the questions and make photocopies to tape above or next to the CD players. At the last station, have a recording of 1 Corinthians 13. It might be a good idea to have a written version that goes along with the CD posted above the player for both visual and audio emphasis.

what to do

At the beginning of the meeting, have the students divide into groups of three or four. Have each group begin at a different CD player station. Tell them to listen to the CD at each station and discuss their answers to the following questions (have the questions photocopied and taped above or next to each player):

- What does the song say about love?
- What is the attitude of the songwriter toward love?

- What action is love taking in the song?

- Does the song describe love as a feeling?

- Is love portrayed as a positive experience or as a problem?

You may add other questions based on the songs you select.

Finally, at the last station where 1 Corinthians 13 is heard, ask the students how this portrayal of love differs from what they have heard in the secular love songs.

This activity can be wrapped up by discussing what the world believes love is and what God says love is. Point out that the world sees love as a feeling that is often temporary and self-centered. Compare this to what God says love is in 1 Corinthians 13. Let the students make conclusions about the difference between the various messages about love.

13

monument reminders

number: **any size group**

prep time: **10-20 minutes**

time required: **30-60 minutes**

In the Bible, there are several incidents of building a monument to honor an important event, such as when Jacob made a monument to remember his covenant with his father-in-law, Laban (see Genesis 31:46), or when God instructed the Israelites to build a monument out of 12 stones after they safely crossed the Jordan River (see Joshua 4:1-7). These places were memorialized to remind the Israelites of the special event that took place there. Why not initiate the same practice with your youth as you make trips or go on retreats?

materials needed

Natural materials

preparation

Gather the materials needed to make the monument. If you choose one of the variations, make sure you have the required materials.

what to do

Gather some rocks, sticks or other natural items with which you will build an altar to have your closing service. If appropriate, you can dismantle the altar following the service or let it remain for visits in future years. (One youth group did this at the beginning of the summer, and many of the students revisited it over that summer for private prayers.)

This activity will give your group members reminders that focus on the milestones in their spiritual growth. These monumental memories can become sacred reminders of God's continual involvement in their lives. Occasionally asking your students if there are any new spiritual milestones in their lives will emphasize their need to continue to build and grow in their relationships with Him.

variations

➡ Make a steppingstone out of concrete by using a form made out of 2x4s nailed together to make a one- to two-foot square. When it is partially dry, write the date and the event on it. Memorable items may be pressed into the concrete before it is dry. This can be placed in a garden area, used to make a remembrance walk, or can be place in a patio area for youth to gather for special prayer or dedication services. If you plan to keep these for a long time, brush on a good concrete sealer.

- Use clay to make a portable monument, or plaster of paris to make a plaque in a box. The students can decorate the monument by collecting items from the area of the retreat or special event and pressing them into the clay or plaster of paris. The remembrance monument can then be taken back with the group and placed in the youth meeting area.

- Encourage students to make individual monuments for milestones in their own lives. A great time to do this is when a student accepts Christ as Savior or when he or she makes a major commitment to serve the Lord, or a rededication. This can be done by writing the date and mile-stone event on a small stone, or in a small plaque made of clay or plaster of paris.

14

room-sized diary

number: **any size group**

prep time: **10 minutes**

time required: **10 minutes**

This is an ongoing group diary that will be a visible reminder to the youth group throughout the year. Students add to the diary after each meeting, which will give them a sense of where they were, what they have accomplished and where they have gone together during the year. The activity builds community by helping students see how much they are a part of each other's lives.

materials needed

A roll of white paper, the size used in covering tables or bulletin boards
Sturdy tape
Felt-tip pens

preparation

Unroll the large roll of paper and securely tape a continuous strip around the youth room. Because the paper is heavy and will be up for a long time, make certain that it is well attached to the wall with sturdy tape.

what to do

Allow the students time after each meeting or before the next meeting to write short reports on what happened at the meeting or activity. Ask those doing the writing to use their first names or initials to identify themselves and to date their entry. After each group entry, draw a bold, vertical line to separate the dates. Artistic students could also add drawings to the written accounts. Have them add meaningful Scripture verses. At the end of the year, and occasionally throughout the year, have the students stop and look at the various entries and talk about the unexpected nature of life.

tip

This ongoing diary can be used to visually show the group how they are all in this life together, and it can help them recall common experiences.

variations

- Add prayer requests that can be identified with big, stick-on dots. Record answers to the prayer requests.

- Award various wacky prizes—perhaps each quarter—to the funniest, strangest, or most touching entries along the way.

- Add a few photos to the diary.

15

round table roulette

number: **any size group**

prep time: **30-60 minutes**

time required: **60-90 minutes**

This group builder will require about 90 minutes to play it properly. It is an eight-round mingling of twosomes, foursomes, open table discussions and entire group responses. In each of the eight rounds, students will be required to take part in a time of sharing or discussion to complete the round. Between the rounds, the leaders, timekeepers or emcee may invite some "from the floor" responses.

materials needed

Five round tables
Chairs
An instruction sheet for each student
A stopwatch
A loud bell, gong or a pan with a wooden spoon
Paper and pencil

preparation

Set up five round tables numbered 1 through 5 with several chairs arranged around each. Rectangular tables are fine if you don't have round ones. On each table, list in large print on a piece of paper the three topics that will be discussed at that table (see Round 4 explanation below). Prepare the questions for Rounds 4, 5 and 8 and also the instruction sheets for students. Select someone to be the timekeeper who will also give the signal to stop or change.

how to begin

Begin by asking the group to sit down to hear the instructions. Read the following introduction:

> Tonight we are going to have fun, but having fun depends on each of you. To make this a success, you need to be willing to share a bit about yourself with others in a safe, non-judgmental way. You'll be

asked to move around the room and meet new people and get to know old friends better. What you share is voluntary and not threatening. By the end of the evening, you'll know more about each other and, hopefully, have made some new friends.

Distribute the Round Table Roulette instruction sheets, and then tell the students that you will lead them through each round—the sheets are simply for reference. Remind them that they need to move quickly at each new round.

the rounds

round 1 (two minutes)

Have the students quickly divide into pairs, preferably with someone they do not know at all or at least not very well. Tell them to each share for their first 30 seconds about their favorite childhood pet and their second 30 seconds about a favorite vacation spot. They should each talk for 30 seconds on each of the topics. Tell the students that you will ring a bell (or a gong or bang a pan) every 30 seconds, at which point they must stop talking and change talkers and/or topics. Each time you give the signal, shout out the reminder of who should be talking and the topic they should be addressing. The whole round should last two minutes.

round 2 (four minutes)

In this round, each duo teams up with another duo to make a foursome. Each of the four should then share for 60 seconds about the following:

- Something neat about their childhood
- A favorite grade-school memory
- Something they really like about their favorite teacher

Ring the bell every 60 seconds and remind them to change talkers. The round should take four minutes.

round 3 (four minutes)

Each duo trades partners within the foursome, creating a new duo. The new duos share the following for two minutes:

- What life was like in their hometowns as children
- How their family life was while they were growing up
- Their favorite hobbies/interests when they were younger

Ring the bell every two minutes, reminding them to change talkers. The entire round should last four minutes.

round 4 (approximately five minutes)

The following rounds will take place at the five round tables. At your five table stations, write a large number, from one to five, on a sheet of 8.5x11-inch paper and put it on the table. Then, on three different colored sheets of paper, write the three topics for that table, depending on the round (Round 4 topics on blue paper, Round 5 topics on yellow paper and Round 8 topics on green paper).

You can allow students to choose the topics of interest to them. If this results in students choosing topics according to what their friends choose, you might want to have them pick numbers or count off by fives. Each table should have an adult discussion leader to facilitate the topic with easy questions and ideas.

If students are allowed to choose a topic of interest to them, you must reserve the right to "redistribute the wealth" of students. Allow the students five minutes or so to talk per round, but ring the bell well before their interest wanes.

On blue paper (8.5x11-inch is fine), the following topics should be written down for Round 4:

Table 1: What is faith?
Table 2: What do you think about current world political events?
Table 3: What is your personal philosophy of life?
Table 4: What is wrong with the world?
Table 5: What is right with the world?

These topics may be adapted to your group's needs, interests or the theme of the meeting, but make the topics fairly equal and representative of the interests of the students, or one table may have 90 percent of the group and others may be empty.

round 5 (five to eight minutes)

On each of the five yellow sheets of paper, the following topics should be written for Round 5:

Table 1: Current movies
Table 2: Current TV shows
Table 3: Talk show host

Table 4: Sports teams
Table 5: Singer or songwriter

Prepare a few leading questions for adult table leaders to spark the discussion. For example: Which is your favorite movie (TV show, talk show host, sports team, singer or songwriter) and why? Which is the worst movie (TV show, talk show host, sports team, singer or songwriter) and why? What did you watch on TV last night? Was it worth your time? Who's your favorite person on your favorite sports team?

Ring the bell after about five to eight minutes. Monitor the discussions to ensure that the students are still on target. If a group is in a jam, assign the table discussion leader some rescue questions to keep the discussion rolling.

round 6 (four minutes)
Next, have everyone find his or her original partner from the first duo and leave the table area. Give each partner two minutes to catch up and report on the interesting things that he or she may have learned or heard in Rounds 3 through 5. Ring the bell every two minutes and remind the groups to change talkers.

round 7 (eight minutes)
Have students return to their original foursome from Round 2 and discuss the following:

- Ideas for a closer walk with Christ
- Ideas for strengthening the youth program
- What they like best about the youth group

Ask one student in each foursome to take notes on ideas, complaints, concerns and joys. Be sure to collect their notes. Ring the bell every two minutes and remind them to change talkers.

round 8 (approximately five minutes)
For this round, the groups will return to the table topics. On each of five green sheets of paper the following topics should be written:

Table 1: The best thing about being a teenager
Table 2: The greatest problem troubling our society
Table 3: What you are learning about Jesus

Table 4: What God has been teaching you recently
Table 5: How you are successfully dealing with your parents

Ring the bell after five minutes. Before closing the meeting, gather the group in a prayer circle and thank God for the varieties of human beings, human experiences and the ability to share our lives with others along this faith walk.

tip

Incidentally, this activity works famously during winter break meetings of college-age students who have not seen each other for some time. It also serves as a good kickoff for a retreat.

Round Table Roulette Instruction Sheet

Each time you hear the bell ring, stop talking and listen for directions.

round 1 (two minutes)
Form pairs and discuss each of the following topics for 30 seconds:

- A favorite childhood pet
- A favorite vacation spot

When you hear the signal, stop talking and listen for instructions.

round 2 (four minutes)
Team up with another pair to make a foursome. Each of you shares for 60 seconds on one of the following topics:

- Something neat about your childhood
- A favorite grade-school memory
- Something you really like about your favorite teacher

When you hear the signal, stop talking and listen for instructions.

round 3 (four minutes)
Trade partners within your foursome, creating new pairs. Each partner shares on the following for two minutes each:

- What life was like in your hometown as a child
- How your family life was while growing up
- Your favorite hobbies/interests when you were younger

When you hear the signal, stop talking and listen for instructions.

round 4 (approximately five minutes)
Choose one of the table topics listed on the blue sheets at each table. Join the group at that table to discuss your topic:

Table 1: What is faith?
Table 2: What do you think about current world political events?
Table 3: What is your personal philosophy of life?

Table 4: What is wrong with the world?
Table 5: What is right with the world?

When you hear the signal, stop talking and listen for instructions.

round 5 (five to eight minutes)

Choose one of the table topics listed on the yellow sheet. Join the group at that table to discuss the topic.

Table 1: Current movies
Table 2: Current TV shows
Table 3: Talk show hosts
Table 4: Sports teams
Table 5: Singer or songwriter

When you hear the signal, stop talking and listen for instructions.

round 6 (two minutes)

Find your first partner, pair up and discuss interesting things you've learned or heard in any of your discussions. When you hear the signal, stop talking and listen for instructions.

round 7 (eight minutes)

Return to your original foursome and discuss the following: (1) ideas for a closer walk with Christ; (2) ideas for strengthening the youth program; (3) what they like best about the youth group. Have one person in your foursome write down ideas. When you hear the signal, stop talking and listen for instructions.

round 8 (approximately five minutes)

Choose one of the table topics listed on the green sheet. Join the group at that table to discuss the topic.

Table 1: The best thing about being a teenager
Table 2: The greatest problem troubling our society
Table 3: What you are learning about Jesus
Table 4: What God has been teaching you recently
Table 5: How you are successfully dealing with your parents

When you hear the signal, stop talking and listen for instructions.

number: **any size group**

prep time: **none**

time required: **5 minutes**

16

secret ID

Teenagers are often fascinated by the accounts of the Early Church gathering for worship during persecution under threat of death or arrest. They seem to love the idea that early believers used the sign of the fish drawn in the sand as a means of identification with the Body of Christ before entering a worship service.

Your students can invent a similar identification symbol for access to youth group meetings. The symbol may change from group to group and from year to year, but the point is that students will be able to say, "I am part of this group because I know the secret entry symbol." Guests and visitors are exempted from this ritual—but this is a great way to let them know they are part of the group when they return and are admitted using the sign.

The sign should be created by the students themselves—a secret handshake, walking into the meeting room backward, a symbol or letter drawn with a fingertip on the back of the entry guard, one sleeve rolled up—just as long as it is their idea.

Historically, such gestures held great meaning and confirmed that the person was indeed a part of the group. Students need to be assured of membership and their identity in any group. This is one small way of giving that security.

17

seven stations mixer

number: **any size group**

prep time: **30 minutes**

time required: **60-90 minutes**

This building activity gathers players into shared responses to seven questions. Then, in the group, they share a few more details of why they answered as they did.

materials needed

Seven 8.5x11-inch pieces of paper
Felt-tip pens
Photocopies of the questions you develop

preparation

Prepare the room for this activity by taping the numbers 1 through 7 on the walls around the room on 8.5x11-inch pieces of paper. These numbers indicate the seven stations that will correspond to the answers of each question. Prepare a sheet with a set of seven questions with seven answers for each question. These questions can be lead-ins for your meeting theme. Make photocopies of the question sheets, one for each student attending.

what to do

As the students gather, give everyone a sheet of questions and a pen or pencil. Explain that they are to answer the questions quietly at their seats without talking to anyone else. Don't tell them about the numbers on the wall, or some students will answer the questions identically so that they can stand together with their friends when the answers are being shared. Give the students a few minutes to answer each of the seven questions.

After they have completed the questions, ask all of the students who answered the first question with answer 1 to stand under the number 1, all of the students who answered the first question with answer 2 to stand under the number 2, and so on through answer 7. Once they are at the stations, instruct each person to share why he or she answered as he or she did. Here is a sample question:

Circle the person who most supported you as you were growing up:

1. Your mom
2. Your dad
3. Your grandma
4. Your grandpa
5. A sibling
6. A neighbor
7. A friend

After the students gather at the number that corresponds to their answers, they will discuss why this person was such a great support. For example, all of the students who gather under number 4 will tell why grandpa was such a great support.

Follow this same procedure with the rest of the questions and answers.

Questions can be about anything: hobbies, politics, Bible characters, sports, pets, and so forth. They can be serious or trivial. What is important is that the questions bring the group to a new level of sharing and understanding and give them new topics of common interest with one another.

18

small-group questions

Choose a Scripture verse, a news item, a quote or any single topic question. Place the students in small groups with four to six members and have them discuss it. This could be done in place of a warm-up activity or a meeting opening by immediately assigning students to small groups as they walk into the room. It is a good alternative to letting them gather and chat and staying only in groups of friends. Let the groups discuss for no more than 10 minutes, or the novelty will wear off.

number: **any size group**

prep time: **1-5 minutes**

time required: **10 minutes**

number: **any size group**

prep time: **variable**

time required: **60+ minutes**

19

special interest groups

Some years ago, a youth pastor responded to the many wishes of his youth groups to give group guitar lessons. Originally, it began as a way for him to meet the insistent wishes of the students in one fell swoop. However, it quickly became something more—it enhanced the youth group and provided a service for the church.

Guitar Choir now meets every Monday for one hour after school throughout the school year. The lessons are free, but the youth pastor teaches the students basic guitar skills with the understanding that because his time is valuable, there needs to be a fair payback. The payback results in something the students really enjoy—playing guitar as a group for various church events.

Guitar Choir plays for the regular worship services, Youth Sunday and the annual church business meeting. They accompany the youth pastor on visits to the early childhood Sunday School classes and Children's Chapel. The Guitar Choir plays when the youth visit soup kitchens or other churches. The choir also leads the singing time at youth group meetings. Of course, the selection of songs is equal to the skills of the students involved, but the congregation and the students don't know the difference.

The ministry of the Guitar Choir has seen miraculous results. Junior and senior high students have begun to step out as leaders as they have gained confidence in learning a skill and performing for others. The Guitar Choir has become a great example of how a ministry can succeed by using the various spiritual gifts of the group members. It also gives students a feeling of belonging to the whole church body when they can be integrated into its ministries in some way.

Guitar Choir has also been a wonderful tool for community evangelism among the unchurched youth. Students bring their guitar-playing friends to join the group. Not surprisingly, many students who have trouble asking a friend to church have no difficulty asking a friend to come play guitar.

Special interest groups within the youth group, such as a Guitar Choir, have strong unity-building effects. The small-group setting has long been recognized for building community, as it builds a bridge into the whole group. The challenge of learning a task together is also a bonding agent. Serving others through what is being learned is a great way to incorporate a sense of ministry. And students who don't shine in any other areas often find a home in the youth group through the Guitar Choir.

You can adapt this Guitar Choir philosophy to any area of skill or ability you or other youth workers have. One youth worker uses the same idea with a leaded glass crafts group he leads. It takes little imagination to come up with other applications.

Here are some suggestions for variations:

Vocal Choir
Service/Missions Group
Drama Club
Computer Club
Puppeteers
Community Service Group
Combined Performance Groups
Sports Teams
Cooking School
Aerobics Class
Hiking Club
Any Craft or Hobby
Nature/Environmental Group
Individual Sports (tennis, golf, and so forth)

number: **any size group**

prep time: **none**

time required: **15-20 minutes**

20

your eulogy

This activity takes about two minutes to introduce, five minutes for each participant to complete, and about 10 minutes (depending on group size) to complete.

materials needed

Paper
Pens or pencils

what to do

Begin by stating the following:

> How do you want to be remembered? Strangely enough, folks who have achieved great deeds in life often reflect that their accomplishments don't fully express who they really are inside—only what they have done.
>
> A "eulogy" is a message shared at a funeral that serves to remind the gathered mourners about the life of the person who has died. Eulogies summarize the person's life by sharing what he or she is likely to be remembered for.
>
> What should be said about your life thus far? What do you believe and stand for? What is important to you? This is your chance to tell us who you really are by writing your own eulogy. Be honest and open and don't hold back. This isn't boasting—it's honestly evaluating how you see yourself and who you are on the inside.

Distribute pens or pencils and paper. Give the students a few minutes to write a short eulogy. Allow time for each person to share his or her eulogy.

variation

Have students write inscriptions for their tombstones. Ask, "If you lived your life the way you would like to, how would you like to be remembered by those whose lives you touch? What would you like to have inscribed on your tombstone?" Give students a few minutes to write their inscriptions, and then have a time of group sharing.

topical guide

GAMES

volunteer games

ICEBREAKERS

crowdbreakers

community builders

preparation times

GAMES

ICEBREAKERS